MW01137087

GIVING OUTSIDE THE BOX

GENEROUS NOW. RICH FOREVER.

DALE LOSCH

Crossworld
Kansas City, Missouri

Giving Outside the Box

Dale Losch

10000 N. Oak Trafficway, Kansas City, MO 64155, USA

Printed in the United States of America
ISBN-9798664803631

Cover design by Ken Cadinouche
Cover image by Matt Vasquez/Lightstock
Photography by Paige Brooks

Visit our website at crossworld.org.

Dale and Jerusha Losch

Dedicated to my wife, Jerusha, whose generosity, godliness, and contentment have brought great gain to our lives.

And dedicated to my children, the original reason I began to put into writing the lessons God was teaching us about giving. I'm thankful for each of you and your spouses: Joel and Kelsey, Jessica and Ken, Nathan and Breanna, Hannah and Joel.

May we all experience the incredible journey of a generous life that makes many rich forever.

CONTENTS

PART 2
Grace Giving: Free to Give More or Free to Not Give?
The Freedom of Giving in the Age of Grace

PART 3
Growth Giving: Amazing Adventure or Impossible Dream?
The Incredible Returns on a Generous Life

PREFACE

I began this writing project about fifteen years ago as a series of lessons to share with my then-teenaged children. The more I learned, the more I wrote. The more I wrote, the more excited I became about sharing it with others. Several times in the past few years I thought it was time to turn it into a book, only to set it aside for more pressing matters. Late in 2019 I decided it was time to make the final push to the finish line in hopes of having it in print by the following year. And today, just as I'm about to break the tape and hand the manuscript off to be edited and published, the world finds itself on the precipice of another financial meltdown.

The year 2020 has become the year of the coronavirus, also known as COVID-19. Between March 2 and April 6 in 2020, North American stock markets shed 35 percent of their value, and there are indications that it's not over yet.[1] Someday it may be little more than a small blip on the radar screen of history but, for the moment, it feels to some a bit like the end of the world. This may be the worst time in recent history to publish a book on generous giving.

Then again, this may be the best time this book could ever come out. Read on and you'll understand why. But let me give you the short version here.

God is not looking for people of great wealth. He's looking for people of great faith. He's not looking for people who will give Him their excess. He's looking for people who will give even to the point of becoming poor, just as Christ did, so that others might become rich (2 Corinthians 8:9). He has, in fact, "chosen the poor of this world to be rich in faith" (James 2:5, NKJV).

A poor widow in Jesus's day out-gave all the wealthy worshipers at the temple with her two small coins. In return, she received the eternal commendation of God.

Another widow from centuries before, poverty-stricken and on the brink of death, sustained God's prophet Elijah and, in the process, miraculously sustained herself and her son.

And some penniless, faith-filled Christ-followers in Macedonia inspired generosity in believers much wealthier than themselves and, as my story will bear out, in my wife and me as well.

People with few resources have an incredible track record of being great givers.

By the time this book is in your hands, the world may be a markedly different place than it was in 2019 when the United States was enjoying unprecedented prosperity. It may be years before we recover.

On the other hand, maybe COVID-19 will be in the rearview mirror. A vaccine or treatment will have been found, the fears of 2020 will have been put to rest, and the world will have moved on.

Either way, the message of this book will be relevant. It is relevant to those who are rich, and to those who are not. It is written for those whose storehouses are full, and for those whose pockets are empty. It's not your net worth that determines how wealthy you will be forever. It's what you do with what you have right now.

"For you know the grace of our Lord Jesus Christ, that though He was rich, yet for your sake He became poor, so that you through His poverty might become rich" (2 Corinthians 8:9, NASB). ■

INTRODUCTION:

THE MESSAGE THAT CHANGED EVERYTHING

Two things happened on June 5, 1982, that forever changed my life. The first was to walk the aisle with the woman I am still happily in love with—Jerusha Ann. The second, and the subject of this book, was a decision we made that would deeply impact how we viewed and used the resources God would entrust to us.

The seed of the second decision was planted one Sunday morning in El Cajon, California, five months before our wedding. That morning, Dr. David Jeremiah, pastor of the church to which Jerusha belonged, shared a message that transformed the way we viewed and managed our resources. It was the apostle Paul's challenge recorded in 2 Corinthians 8:7 that grabbed our attention: "But since you *excel* in everything—in faith, in speech, in knowledge, in complete earnestness and in the love we have kindled in you—see that you also *excel* in this grace of giving" (emphasis mine).

Imagine a believer asserting he had finally arrived in his pursuit of faith or love: "Friends, listen. I have arrived at the pinnacle of perfect love. There is no room for improvement."

We would consider such a person to be either extremely proud or delusional. No one in this life will ever come to the point where they have no more room for growth in faith, speech, knowledge, love, or any other number of Christian graces. Yet, according to Paul, the same principle applies to the grace of giving. He said believers should grow in their giving capacity, just as in other areas of their Christian development.

Some Exceptional Givers

Paul was not simply urging the believers in Corinth to be more generous. He was urging them to imitate a particular group of people whose generosity had become legendary. Who were these people? They were not doctors, lawyers, and CEOs as we might expect—those we assume could afford to be generous because of their sizable incomes. No, these were some of the poorest of the poor. These were a group of believers in the region of Macedonia whom Paul described as being in "extreme poverty." On top of that, they had experienced "a severe test of affliction" (2 Corinthians 8:2, ESV). Apparently, they had suffered much for their faith in Christ.

Yet these people led the way in their outpouring of generosity toward fellow believers in Jerusalem for whom Paul was collecting an offering. They gave so generously in spite of their own difficult circumstances that Paul told the believers in Corinth about them: "We want you to know… about the grace of God that has been given among the churches of Macedonia," he wrote. "For they gave according to their means… and beyond their means…" (vv. 1, 3). These were poor people who were rich in the grace of giving.

It seems Paul hadn't even expected them to participate in the offering. He wrote, "They did it of their own accord, begging us earnestly for the favor of taking part…" (vv. 3, 4). Perhaps he assumed they needed it as much as the intended recipients. Maybe, knowing their poverty, he felt too embarrassed to even approach them. Whatever his thinking, the Macedonians ended up begging Paul to let them participate in the offering. And what they gave astounded him. He admitted that it was "not as we expected" (v. 5). So amazed was he at their exceptional giving that he held them up as a model for others.

But, as exemplary as they were, they were not the ultimate model. Paul then pointed to Jesus Himself—"For you know the grace of our Lord Jesus Christ, that though He was rich, yet for your sake He became poor, so that you through His poverty might become rich" (2 Corinthians 8:9, NASB).

Paul took the greatest act in all of history—the self-emptying, redemptive work of Jesus Christ—and held it up as a model for financial generosity. Think about that: The cross is the model for how we should use our money. Jesus, the supreme "rich man," became the ultimate "poor man" so that untold billions of spiritually "poor" lost sinners could become eternally "rich." That truth, said Paul, should inform our giving.

Following the Leaders

In his message that day in 1982, Dr. Jeremiah challenged people to become growing givers. For some reason, Jerusha's heart and mine were ripe on that day for that truth. We soon began to discover that giving a *tithe*—10 percent of one's income—was just the beginning of an incredible journey God would take us on. Since that day, our hunger to apply the scriptural admonition by following the example of the generous Macedonians and of Jesus Himself has become one of the greatest sources of blessing in our married life.

Before we walked the aisle, we agreed that our wedding anniversary would become the date of an annual giving review at which time we would ask ourselves two simple questions. For more than thirty-five years now, those questions, and our answers to them have profoundly impacted our lives, releasing us to discover the freedom of an increasingly generous lifestyle. ■

Growing Outside the Box

"Be doers of the Word, and not hearers only" (James 1:22).

1. Think of an example of something you have *excelled* in; in other words, something at which you became *excellent*. How did you achieve excellence in that aspect of your life?

2. What would it look like for you to "excel in this grace of giving" (2 Corinthians 8:7)? What's one thing you could begin doing that would nudge you in the direction of *excelling* in generosity?

3. Take a few minutes to read 2 Corinthians 8:1–9 and give some thought to the following questions:

    - Why do you think the Macedonians in poverty had such a strong desire to give?
    - What does it mean to give "beyond one's ability"? When can you remember doing that? What did it feel like?
    - What appears to be the connection between giving our resources to others and giving ourselves to God?
    - How is the redemptive work of Christ meant to be a model to us in the matter of giving?

PART 1

TO GIVE OR NOT TO GIVE: BLESSING OR CURSE?

The Foundations of Giving

1 THE STORY OF THE RED BOX

My parents believed in giving. From the very beginning, they taught my siblings and me that giving a tenth of our income back to God was not optional for a follower of Jesus. So, from my earliest recollections, I gave to God a tenth of everything I received, whether from my weekly allowance or the money I earned from shoveling snow and cutting lawns.

The most powerful teaching method, however, came not by way of parental exhortation but by example. Every week as Sunday approached, my father would open the cupboard above the kitchen stove and take out a red metal recipe box that had been designated to hold the family tithe. That money was placed into a church envelope that was then given to my mother, whose job it was to place it in the offering each Sunday. It was her job for the simple reason that my father, as the pastor, apparently didn't want to make a public display of his giving from his position at the front of the church.

When I was about age ten, my dad assigned to me the task of preparing that envelope. I'm not sure why he did this, but maybe he understood the teaching value of that exercise. For the next five years or so, it became my job every Sunday morning to take the money from the little red box in the cupboard and put it in the numbered church envelope.

Two things strike me about that experience. First, I never remember the box being empty on Sunday morning. I don't know when he put the money in, but it was always there. Second, the amount remained constant with occasional increases whenever my father received a pay raise. I don't remember a specific dollar figure except the amount from the last year I remember doing it as a fifteen-year-old: forty dollars. Every Sunday, forty dollars went from the red metal box to the white numbered envelope to the brown wooden offering plate. My parents not only taught us to tithe, they modeled it.

Two Questions

When Jerusha told me about Dr. Jeremiah's message from 2 Corinthians 8, the concept of giving a tenth of our income to God was already a part of my Christian DNA. But Pastor Jeremiah was talking about something different—not just tithing but growing. If God desired for us to grow in giving, just as in other Christian graces such as love and faith, then giving ten percent was only the beginning. From childhood I had learned to give the ten percent that was "inside the box." Now it was time to start giving "outside the box."

After some discussion, we decided to ask ourselves two questions on each wedding anniversary. First, "Has God been faithful this past year to provide for all our needs when we gave Him *x* percent?" If yes, then we would ask the second: "Can we trust God by increasing our giving in the coming year to *y* percent?"

For our entire married life up to the present day, the answer to the first question has always been a resounding yes! God has always met our needs and, in most cases, far more than our needs. Consequently, every year we have not only asked the second question, but have usually answered it in the affirmative, trusting God to help us take our giving to a new level. With few exceptions, by His grace, we have met those objectives, often with astounding results. Time after time we have experienced the reality of God's promise in Malachi 3:10.

> "'Bring the whole tithe into the storehouse, that there may be food in my house. Test me in this,' says the LORD Almighty, 'and see if I will not throw open the floodgates of heaven and pour out so much blessing that there will not be room enough to store it.'"

I am convinced many believers are missing out on one of the most exciting adventures in life because they have never put God to the test in the matter of generous giving. Though it's hard to believe, every poll on the giving patterns of North Americans pegs the median giving at between 2 and 4 percent of their total income. A report by empty tomb, inc., found that evangelical Christians in America give about 4 percent of their income to charities and that the broader Christian community gives an average of 2.43 percent.[2]

If this is true, then the floodgates of heaven must be bulging to the breaking point, waiting for people who have yet to take God at His word. ■

Growing Outside the Box

"Be doers of the Word, and not hearers only" (James 1:22).

1. What have been the most formative influences, positive or negative, in developing your attitudes and practices in relation to giving?
2. Do you believe the Old Testament practice of giving a tenth of our income back to God is something God desires of New Testament believers? Why or why not?
3. Regardless of what you may currently think about the practice of tithing, how important is it, in your opinion, that a Christian grow in their giving? Explain.
4. Write one thing each of the following verses teaches about giving.
    - "It is more blessed to give than to receive" (Acts 20:35).
    - "Give, and it will be given to you. A good measure, pressed down, shaken together and running over, will be poured into your lap. For with the measure you use, it will be measured to you" (Luke 6:38).

2 IS IT REALLY MORE BLESSED TO GIVE?

I have always felt a great degree of freedom in preaching and teaching on the topic of money. Perhaps it's because for most of my years in vocational Christian ministry, I have not been salaried by any one church and thus had no worries that my audience might assume I stood to directly benefit from what I was saying.

Unfortunately, some pastors do not always feel the same degree of freedom. Because financial matters are so much a part of our existence, addressing the issue of money and possessions is sometimes perceived as meddling. Recently I visited a church where the pastor was beginning a three-week series on financial stewardship. To my dismay, he apologized to visitors that they had happened to come on one of the few Sundays that he ever addresses this topic.

I'm thankful Dr. Jeremiah didn't flinch back in 1982 when it came to declaring to God's people what the Bible had to say about giving. Nor has he been afraid to do so since. Instead, from the first year that he began as the pastor of what is now Shadow Mountain Community Church, he has given the first month of every year to teaching his congregation on biblical stewardship. And he makes no apologies.

Why apologize for something God commends and blesses? God so loves generous givers that we should be telling people *how fortunate they are* to arrive on the Sunday we're teaching on it. Yet more than a few pastors confess the topic of giving is avoided at all costs, preferring to let a visiting speaker do the honors or, worse yet, to avoid the subject altogether.

To hear such sentiments, one might be inclined to think giving is not all the Bible makes it out to be—that it's a lot of hype, rather than a source of untold blessing. Some believers seem to view giving like they do a visit to the doctor with their four-year-old child. The child is told the needle will hardly be felt at all—that it's just a tiny pinprick followed by a lollypop or an ice cream cone. But the reality is that it hurts a whole lot and the promised treats are simply a diversionary tactic.

In a similar way, some people view giving as a lot more pain than pleasure. Though they can't deny that it is clearly taught in Scripture, they're not so sure it will be a positive experience. And any attempt to extol its virtues is viewed as simply sugar-coating a truth that, in reality, is a bitter pill to swallow.

Some Unbelievable Promises

I can assure you I am not writing about giving because I need someone to pay my salary or because I stand to profit by convincing people to swallow a sugar-coated pill that is bitter at its core. Rather, it is because I have discovered that the benefits of generous giving are so much greater than any possible disadvantages that I genuinely love to tell others about it. God's promises concerning giving are so many and so overwhelmingly positive that I am amazed to encounter believers who don't take them seriously.

More Blessed to What?

One of those amazing promises of Scripture is so well known that even many non-religious people recognize these words: "It is more blessed to give than to receive." It's intriguing to note that while Jesus was the one who spoke those words, they are nowhere found in the Gospel accounts. So how do we know He said them? The answer comes from the Book of Acts where the apostle Paul attributed those words to Jesus, saying to the leaders of the church in Ephesus: "In everything I did, I showed you that by this kind of hard work we must help the weak, remembering the words the Lord Jesus himself said: 'It is more blessed to give than to receive'" (Acts 20:35).

These words of Christ were apparently so familiar and accepted by the early church as having come from the lips of Christ that Paul did not need to defend their origin. Jesus had obviously said them so frequently that anyone who knew anything about Jesus recognized these words as having originated with Him.

If we are to take these words at face value, they represent one of the greatest pleasures available to mankind—better even than the pleasure of receiving. Think about that. Most people enjoy being on the receiving end of good things. I know I do. One of my favorite times of year is tax time. I genuinely look forward to filing my return, not because I like taxes, but because I always receive a refund from the government. I love it when the government returns my hard-earned money. But that's just the beginning. I also enjoy receiving a wide variety of other good things—like compliments on a job well done, back massages from my kids, home-cooked meals from my wife, front row seats at a sporting event, and first place in anything that remotely involves competition. Don't kid yourself—receiving is fantastic. How else to explain the crowds of shoppers who line up by the thousands in the wee hours of the morning on the day *after* Christmas? It's not because they want to *give* a little more. It's because they love receiving.

But Jesus essentially said: "If you think receiving is fun, just wait till you get the hang of giving. Giving is even better!" The following true story demonstrates how enjoyable giving can be.

In early December 2019, a man named Jack and his family prepared to board an overnight international flight to New York City. Before boarding the plane, Jack had struck up an instant friendship with Violet, an eighty-eight-year-old woman waiting for the same flight. It must've been there that he learned of his new friend's wish and then determined to make it come true.

After boarding, Jack left his spacious seat in first class and walked the long aisle to find Violet seated in economy class next to the restrooms. Jack offered to trade places with Violet for the flight—or rather, his first-class bed for her non-reclining seat—and she accepted. Her wish to fly in style had come true.

Flight attendant Leah Amy witnessed it all and later wrote on Facebook that Jack "never made a peep or asked for anything the rest of the flight. No fuss, no attention. He literally did it out of the kindness of his own heart...."

Speaking of Violet's reaction, Leah added, "You should [have] seen her face when I tucked her in bed after supper."[3] As much as Violet was blessed by that act of generosity, I suspect Jack was even more blessed. He experienced the reality of what Jesus said two thousand years ago about giving being greater than receiving. Jesus wasn't speaking in hyperbole. He really meant it. Do we believe it?

Running Over

More of Jesus's amazing words about giving and receiving are recorded for us in Luke 6. It is interesting these particular words were spoken on the heels of another familiar Scripture, known to Christians and non-Christians alike. Though some would not be able to identify the author, most westerners are well-acquainted with this proverb: "Do unto others as you would have them do unto you." These were Jesus's words, found in verse 31. In context, Christ was making a series of statements that flew in the face of the commonly held wisdom of the day. For instance, whoever heard teaching to "bless those who curse you" (v. 28) or to "lend... without expecting to get anything back" (v. 35)? So, when Jesus spoke the words in verse 38, His listeners must have been equally puzzled: "Give, and it will be given to you. A good measure, pressed down, shaken together and running over, will be poured into your lap. For with the measure you use, it will be measured to you."

Wouldn't you love to do your shopping at a store where the clerk tried to give you as much for your money as he possibly could? Where he sold you a pound and a quarter of fresh ground coffee for the price of a pound, simply because he wanted to fill the bag to bulging?

My wife sometimes goes to the local farmers market to buy our fruit and vegetables. On occasion, I go with her. If you're a bargain hunter like me, you will understand that I don't simply buy from the first stand I come to. I approach shopping much like I do a competitive sport. The goal is not simply to get the product, but to get the best possible deal in the entire market. If I'm looking for golden delicious apples, I consider that I have won only when I have located the best bargain among all the vendors. When I find the best price, I then select the container that looks the fullest. But imagine my surprise and pleasure if, when the vendor lifted the plastic sack out of the bushel basket, he topped it with another twelve or fifteen apples because the bag still had room. That seller would immediately become my vendor of choice.

The audience of Jesus's day was accustomed to marketplace shopping where the use of scales and measures was standard practice. Dishonest vendors would sometimes have two sets of weights and measures, one that was true, the other false. When an unsuspecting buyer was making his purchase, the crooked merchant would reach into his bag of weights and take out one that was lighter than its purported weight, thus cheating the customer out of an ounce or two of product. The same was true of the containers with which he measured product sold by volume rather than weight. A slightly undersized measure increased the profit margin of a dishonest seller.

This was such common practice in the ancient world that the Mosaic Law addressed the issue in these terms:

> "Do not have two differing weights in your bag—one heavy, one light. Do not have two differing measures in your house—one large, one small. You must have accurate and honest weights and measures, so that you may live long in the land the LORD your God is giving you" (Deuteronomy 25:13–15).

Another translation calls it "a full and just measure" (v. 15, NASB). The Law called for honesty in one's business dealings, but Jesus took the principle of using a "full and just measure" and raised it to an unheard-of level. A merchant who would not only use a "good measure" but would also make it "pressed down, shaken together and running over" (Luke 6:38) was something one only dreamed of.

This was the image Jesus chose to describe the standard God would use with those who are generous. His words are nothing short of spectacular. If they were the only ones of their kind in Scripture, I might be tempted to search for another explanation of their meaning. But they are not isolated words. Scripture is full, from beginning to end, with many similar claims. Furthermore, if I had not personally experienced the reality of these words in my own life, I would undoubtedly ignore them, or might look for some contextual reason why they were not intended for believers throughout the ages. But neither my experience nor my commitment to rightly interpret Scripture will allow me to do that. I have discovered the reality of these promises of God in so many instances in my life that I cannot help but believe Jesus meant exactly what He said.

They Will Pour into Your Lap

A number of years ago, Jerusha and I marked our nineteenth anniversary and finished our annual inventory of God's provision in our lives. We then decided to increase our annual giving by one percentage point of our total annual income. At the time, that represented about $600 in increased giving for the year. While this may not seem like a huge amount in and of itself, it seemed like a significant amount to us when we were already giving well beyond the tithe of our income. But God had been faithful in the preceding year to meet all our needs, and so we chose to take another small step of faith.

A few weeks later while on a trip, a friend whom Jerusha hadn't seen in two years invited her out for lunch. Just before parting ways afterward, her friend handed Jerusha an envelope and said, "I want you to have this. It's for you and Dale to use on anything you need." After saying goodbye, Jerusha opened the envelope to discover a check for $1,800! Within less than a month of our commitment to grow a little more in the grace of giving, God had measured back to us triple the increase we had committed.

At this point perhaps you have warning bells going off in your head. "Isn't this the teaching of prosperity theology—give to God, and He'll make you rich?" Not a few television preachers have made a lot of money telling their followers that if they will make a faith gift to the ministry, God will give them back two, three, five, or even ten-fold. So, what's the difference between that and what we're saying here? The answer to that question lies in understanding God's purpose in blessing us. ■

Growing Outside the Box

"Be doers of the Word, and not hearers only" (James 1:22).

1. In what ways have you personally experienced that it is more blessed to give than to receive?
2. How have you experienced the truth that God is able to match or exceed your capacity to give?
3. In light of what God says about the blessings of giving, why do you think so many of His children are not more generous?
4. What might it look like this week to use a good or generous measure toward a person or a ministry you're familiar with?
5. Choose to be generous in at least one such relationship and ask God to help you see how much more blessed it is to be an increasingly generous person.
6. Read 2 Corinthians 9:6–11 and reflect on the following questions in preparation for the next chapter:
    - What was the apostle Paul talking about when he used the illustration of sowing and reaping?
    - Describe the relationship between giving and receiving.
    - What is God's purpose in blessing generous people with more resources?

3 WHY ARE WE SO BLESSED?

Western societies are among some of the most prosperous in the history of the world. Even in difficult economic times, we continue to be affluent compared to most other nations. Why have we been so blessed? A survey taken in the mid-1990s revealed that 70 percent of Americans believed their financial situation indicated, at least in part, God's regard for them.[4] Though today's numbers may not look exactly the same, the basic human belief has not changed. Those who believe in God tend to connect wealth with divine favor.

In other words, we think God blesses us with financial prosperity because He likes us.

This kind of thinking is not much different from what human beings have believed throughout history. Health, wealth, and happiness have long been viewed as signs of God's favor while sickness, financial loss, and general misfortune are considered sufficient reason to question whether we've done something to make God upset with us. In the book of Job, that classic story of suffering and loss, Job's friends immediately jump to that conclusion. They were quick to come up with such encouraging sound bites as: "Those who sow trouble reap it" and "If you are pure and upright… [God will] restore you to your prosperous state" (Job 4:8; 8:6–7). They sincerely believed Job's sin caused his losses and, if Job cleaned up his act, he would get it all back.

Proponents of prosperity theology are not content, however, to merely regard prosperity and well-being as signs of God's pleasure. Instead, they promise that a life of God-given prosperity is guaranteed by taking our resources and giving them to God's cause that, by coincidence, is their ministry. In this system, prosperity is not only the assured result of giving, it is often the goal. One who is not healthy and prosperous is said to be missing out on their God-given destiny.

One well-known American televangelist mailed out an eight-page, full-color appeal claiming "God will make you a thousand times more" if you sent money. It didn't take a rocket scientist to guess what the televangelist had in mind. The final three pages urged the reader to "sow his seed" in the televangelist's ministry which he assured them was "good ground." He then promised a "thousand times more" miracles in the lives of donors.

Blessed to Bless Others

The great danger in the prosperity theology gospel is that it is half right. God does promise, in a general way, to prosper those who are gracious. Jesus's promise to bless givers with an overflowing measure is by no means an isolated instance. Wise and wealthy King Solomon wrote: "Honor the LORD with your wealth, with the firstfruits of all your crops; then your barns will be filled to overflowing..." (Proverbs 3:9–10). God said virtually the same thing through the mouth of Malachi when He promised to "open the floodgates of heaven" if they would simply trust and obey Him in the matter of tithing (Malachi 3:10). The clear teaching of Scripture is that God blesses those who honor Him with their finances.

But Scripture doesn't stop there. God's material blessing was never intended to be an end in itself. God never invites us to give so He can make us rich in the world's wealth. Why then does He offer to bless the generous soul?

In Psalm 67, the writer asked God to bless the nation of Israel with prosperity. "God be gracious to us and bless us and cause His face to shine upon us," he prayed (v. 1, NASB). A simple look around us today quickly confirms we in the West have experienced the answer to that prayer. We are blessed with a spiritual heritage most of the world has never known. We are blessed with financial prosperity unrivaled in the history of the world. We are blessed with peace within our borders, education, health care, food in abundance. The list is endless.

But why has God blessed us? Is it simply because, as many people think, He likes us? Fortunately, the psalm writer does not leave us to guess the answer. The reason he asks for God's blessing on the nation is so "that Your way may be known on earth, Your salvation among all nations" (v. 2). If that isn't clear enough, he says it again at the end of the psalm in plain language: "God blesses us, that all the ends of the earth may fear Him" (v. 7). God does not bless us so we might consume His goodness on ourselves. His blessing on us is connected to His concern for the nations.

Doing Without for Those Without the Gospel

In the late 1800s, British missionary Hudson Taylor returned from China to his homeland to plead with the church to send 100 more workers and to release the resources necessary to send them. It seemed like a monumental task, especially considering he needed 10,000 pounds, roughly $700,000 in today's currency, just to get them there. A special breakfast was organized in London during which one man stood and pulled a letter from his pocket from a poor widow in Scotland who regularly gave from her poverty and who wrote: "I can do without food, but the people of China cannot do without the gospel." So moved was one man by the sacrifice of that poor woman that he stood and said: "I give large sums of money, but what I have given has never cost me a meal." He pledged 500 pounds on the spot—the equivalent of $35,000 today.

Both widow and wealthy man apparently understood that whatever God had blessed them with was not merely because He liked them. He wanted to bless the nations through them. By November of that year, Taylor not only had his 100 new workers, he also had the money in hand to send them to China—$748,000.[5]

A Lesson from Farming

The New Testament illustrates God's purpose in blessing us with an example from the world of agriculture—that of sowing and reaping. Exhorting his readers to participate in an offering that was being taken to relieve the poverty of the believers in Palestine, the apostle Paul wrote to the believers in Corinth: "Whoever sows sparingly will also reap sparingly, and whoever sows generously will also reap generously" (2 Corinthians 9:6). The physical laws of planting and harvesting illustrate the spiritual truth that the size of the yield is directly proportional to the amount that is planted. Paul's illustration comes from the world of agriculture, but he was talking about money and about God's commitment to prosper the giver.

But for what purpose? Why does God promise a multiplied return on our giving? He tells us in verse 10: "He [God] who supplies seed to the sower and bread for food will supply and multiply your seed for sowing and increase the harvest of your righteousness" (ESV). Please notice that God does not multiply our seed for storing, but for sowing. He does not pour out His blessing on givers to make them rich, but rather to make others rich. His abundance is not for those who want to stockpile it but for those who want to distribute it. The glaring error of prosperity theology is that its goal is self-centered. The clear biblical teaching of what we might call "harvest theology" is that it is kingdom-centered, others-centered, and sowing-centered.

God has promised to pour out His abundance, material and spiritual, on those who are committed to sharing His blessing with others. This means those who learn to give generously will generally tend to have resources to give. They may or may not be wealthy, but they will be generous. The reality is that God's greatest givers are not always visibly prosperous. In some cases, they seem to be those who can least afford it.

Givers Don't Always Look the Part

Many will recall the biblical account of the poor widow who came to the temple one day and put into the treasury the last two pennies she owned, while others far wealthier than she were putting in much larger sums. Jesus acknowledged her as the greatest giver of the whole lot when He said she "put more into the treasury than all the others" (Mark 12:43). What made this woman poor? Most likely it was her widowhood rather than her generosity.

Yet, her gift that day is a clear indication that she had learned to be a generous giver long before she ever came down to her last two pennies.

Recently I visited a widow who for many years has financially supported Crossworld, the ministry with which I've served for more than thirty years. She lives in a modest house with her two adopted children. By all appearances she is not a wealthy woman. On that same trip I visited a half dozen others associated with our ministry, all of whom appeared to have significantly more resources at their disposal.

The week after I returned, our ministry's director of donor relations came to my office and said, "You'll never guess who I just had a call from." She proceeded to tell me that the woman of apparent modest means had been deeply moved by the gospel opportunities she had been reading about since my visit. As a result, she wanted to make a five-figure gift to help us engage more unreached people. Some of God's greatest givers don't necessarily look the part.

God's greatest givers do not always appear to be prosperous because God's harvest is not always paid out in dollars and cents. In referring to financial resources, God promised not only increased "seed for sowing" but also an increase in "the harvest of your righteousness" so that we will be "enriched in *every way*" (2 Corinthians 9:10–11,

ESV, emphasis mine). Sometimes my gifts will be multiplied back to me in additional financial resources. Other times the pay-off might be a believer whose heart is encouraged, a cross-cultural worker whose ministry is helped, or a lost person whose eternal destiny is changed.

Generous kingdom giving does not always guarantee I will have a healthy balance in my mutual fund, but it does guarantee I will be "enriched in every way" for the purpose of continued investment of God's resources.

Blessed in Poverty and Prosperity

Over the years, Jerusha and I have known some amazing financial blessings. Even as I write this chapter, we find ourselves in the midst of a particular financial blessing that we could never have imagined possible.

But we have also known lean times. One of those times occurred during my years as a seminary student in Dallas, Texas. Back then, Jerusha earned a modest salary teaching in a Christian elementary school, while I studied full-time at seminary. The cost of my studies ate up about one-third of our income and, at that point in our lives, we were giving 13 percent of our salary to charitable causes. After paying for food, housing, car, and other expenses, we didn't have much disposable income left. As an inexpensive way to pass our free time, we often went for long walks after dinner.

One evening stands out in my memory. It was toward the end of the month and we literally didn't have a single penny left. I desperately wanted to buy Jerusha an ice cream treat at the local Wendy's. But, without a penny to my name and a commitment to not buy on credit, even ice cream was out of the question. So, I decided to pray.

As we walked, I kept silently saying to God, "Lord, please let me find some change on the street so I can buy Jerusha a Wendy's Frosty." As I walked and prayed, I kept my eyes glued to the sidewalk in search of God's answer. Jerusha noticed that my eyes were focused downward instead of ahead.

"Honey, what are you doing?" she asked.

"I'm asking God to help me find some change so I can buy you a Frosty."

At that, she began to laugh, declaring that she'd been doing the same thing. The humor of the situation struck us so hard that we laughed till we cried.

I realize that at this point I'm supposed to tell you of how God miraculously responded to our prayers and provided the ninety-nine cents we needed for two Frosties.

(Yes, you could buy two for that price back then.) But He didn't.

We arrived back at our apartment with no more money than when we had left—but we were richer. Through that lean experience and others like it, we agreed that nothing compares to the lessons we learned, the laughter we shared, and the memories we made. As the apostle Paul wrote to the Philippian believers, "…I have learned to be content whatever the circumstances. I know what it is to be in need, and I know what it is to have plenty…" (Philippians 4:11–12a). A theology of money that does not include ample portions of God-given leanness is a defective theology indeed.

A biblical theology of money is not prosperity focused. It is sowing focused. It is one that recognizes God loves those who give generously, and that He has uniquely committed Himself to prosper such individuals so they can continue to please Him and bless others through their giving.

All this talk of God's blessing on generous givers raises questions:

1. If God loves to bless generous people, why aren't we all more generous?

2. If giving is such a blessing, why does it seem to be such a contentious issue?

To answer these questions, we must see where the idea of biblical giving originated historically and how quickly humanity strayed from God's way. ■

Growing Outside the Box

"Be doers of the Word, and not hearers only" (James 1:22).

1. Why do you think God expresses great love for one who gives generously and cheerfully?
2. What words do you think God would use to describe your giving?
3. Most research on giving patterns shows the less people have, the more proportionally they tend to give. Why do you think this is?
4. Take time to reflect on your own heart attitudes when it comes to giving. How well do they reflect joy and generosity? How well do your giving patterns reflect belief in the amazing promises God makes to those who give generously?
5. Read Genesis 4:1–8 and reflect on the following questions in preparation for the next chapter:
    - How do you think Cain and Abel knew what God expected them to offer back to Him?
    - Compare their two offerings. What do you think made one pleasing to God and the other not pleasing?
    - Is there anything that would indicate joyful, generous giving in either of the offerings? If so, what?

4 MONEY WARS

The giving of a tithe, or 10 percent, to God may feel like an impossibility if you've never done it before. You may be asking yourself, "How could I possibly live on 90 percent of my income when I'm not even making it on 100 percent?" Furthermore, the thought of growing your giving beyond a tithe may also feel impossible. Let me encourage you to hang in there. We'll get there one step at a time.

Tithing is not the home run of biblical giving. In baseball terms, it is probably more like a single. But singles are a great place to start. Baseball games can be won by putting together a good string of singles. So, let's start there. Where did the idea of tithing come from and what makes it so important?

A Contentious Issue

The issue of giving to God has been contentious from the start. In fact, the first recorded fight in history was sparked by the issue of giving and ended in murder.

After Adam and Eve's banishment from the garden, a family conflict erupted over giving. Cain, their eldest son, cultivated the ground. His brother, Abel, raised livestock. Both brothers knew God wanted them to bring Him an offering from the increase of their labors. So, they did. "In the course of time Cain brought some of the fruits of the soil as an offering to the LORD. And Abel also brought an offering—fat portions from some of the firstborn of his flock" (Genesis 4:3, 4a).

However, there was a problem with one of the offerings: "…The LORD looked with favor on Abel and his offering, but on Cain and his offering he did not look with favor" (vv. 4, 5). The original Hebrew word *shah,* translated as *looked,* literally means "to look or gaze with intense interest." God gazed intently and was not impressed with Cain's offering.

God's interest and pleasure in what we offer Him is intriguing. Perhaps the convenient, automated methods of giving, common in western society, have caused us to lose sight of how much giving is an act of worship in which

God takes a personal interest. We might do well to imagine that as we make our gift on Sunday morning, God is, figuratively, leaning in, gazing at what we're offering to Him, and pondering what it reflects about our devotion. Such was the case with Abel's offering and, as God gazed with interest, what He saw pleased Him.

The opposite was true of Cain's offering. God did not gaze on it with favor. He was not pleased.

The fact that something was wrong indicates God had already told them what He expected. If He had not, He would have had no basis for being displeased. Although nothing in these early chapters of Genesis explicitly stated that God had communicated a standard for giving, He obviously had. Perhaps He had spoken to Cain and Abel or to their parents directly on the matter. Indeed, He spoke to Cain concerning his anger, just a few verses later.

From Homage to Homicide

Although Cain knew his sacrifice fell short, he didn't take it well when God spoke to him about it. Worse yet, the text says he was "very angry" and his face became "downcast." Cain's feeling went beyond simple hurt or annoyance. Cain's anger boiled. The original Hebrew word, *charah,* literally means "to burn or glow like a fire."

The matter of giving has always evoked strong reactions for the simple reason that it touches on something near and dear to the hearts of most people: their money. It is exceedingly difficult for us to remain clear-headed and reasonable when someone begins meddling in our material affairs. The number one issue couples fight about is also a topic many couples avoid discussing—money. According to a survey by Ramsey Solutions, money fights are the second leading cause of divorce, behind infidelity."[6]

Money is also the driving force behind most criminal activity such as drug dealing, human trafficking, and murder. And money is near the top of the list when it comes to church conflicts. Not surprisingly then, money was at the root of this historic conflict between two men and their God.

Scripture does not tell us what was wrong with Cain's offering. Some have said God's displeasure stemmed from Cain's bloodless sacrifice that ignored God's requirement for atonement through the shedding of blood (Leviticus 17:11). Others have suggested the problem lay in the disparate quality of the two offerings. While Abel brought the firstborn and the best fatty portions, Cain brought only "some of the fruits of the soil" (v. 3) as opposed to the firstfruits God required.

Whatever the case may be, Cain knew exactly what the problem was. He did not need an explanation from God, nor did he get one. God simply said to him, "If you do what is right, will you not be accepted?" (v. 7). Cain knew what was right, because evidently God had already told him.

But Cain didn't care. He did not like being told what he should or shouldn't give to God. Neither do some people today. So, one day in the field, Cain called Abel out, perhaps muttering under his breath: "If it's the shedding of blood God wants, that's exactly what He'll get." Boiling with anger toward God, Cain took it out on his brother and murdered him. It is hard to believe an act of worship could end so tragically. Yet such is the nature of money's power when it gains the upper hand in our affections.

Back in my early days of pastoral ministry, a certain wealthy man attended my church. One Monday morning after a particularly good Sunday worship experience, a letter arrived on my desk from this man. In it, he blasted the pastoral leadership team for projecting the words of the worship songs up on a screen rather than using the hymnals in the back of each pew. He proceeded to argue that those hymn books contained all the riches of biblical truth set to music. He threatened that, until we agreed to do away with worship from a screen, he would not put his hard-earned money in the offering plate. He turned an act of worship into a money war.

Perhaps it is because of God's understanding of the corrupting power of money that He addresses the issue of giving so early in human history. He understands, as Jesus so clearly articulated several millennia later, that when it comes to material things, "No one can serve two masters, for either he will hate the one and love the other, or he will be devoted to the one and despise the other. You cannot serve God and money" (Matthew 6:24, ESV). The story of Cain and Abel is not only a tragic testimony to the volatility of the human heart when it comes to one's possessions, but it is a clear indication that God gave instructions about giving, right from the start of human history.

God's Old Testament Expectations

God had not simply given Cain and Abel carte blanche to give whatever they wanted, or the option to give nothing at all. What exactly had He told them? What did Cain and

Abel understand about God's expectations for giving? A further look at the Genesis account sheds some light.

Several generations after Adam, God called a man named Abraham to become the father of the nation of Israel. Soon after he arrived in the land of Palestine, his nephew Lot became the victim of a warring king. This monarch came to the city where Lot lived, defeated its king, and carried Lot and his family off as captives.

When word reached Abraham with news of the calamity that had befallen his relative, he cobbled together an army of 318 men and pursued the aggressors. Surprising them in a night raid, Abraham liberated Lot and his family, retrieving all the people and plunder taken in battle.

In Hebrews 7, we learn that when Abraham returned home, Melchizedek, the king of Salem who was also known as a "priest of God Most High" (v. 1), came out to bless him for the victory God had wrought on his behalf. In response to this blessing, Abraham took "a tenth of the plunder" (v. 4) and gave it to God's priest.

Who told Abraham he should do this? And where did he get the figure of 10 percent? Though Scripture had not yet been written, somehow Abraham knew what God expected.

Not only did Abraham know, but so did his family. Years later, another dispute between brothers broke out, again over material things. It happened with Abraham's twin grandsons: Esau, the older and primary heir, and Jacob. Jacob schemed to swindle Esau out of his inheritance rights as well as their father Isaac's final blessing. Jacob ran for his life from his betrayed, angry brother with nothing but the clothes on his back. He cried out to God for safe passage back home, promising, "then the LORD will be my God… and of all that you give me I will give you a tenth" (Genesis 28:21–22).

Here was a man who had apparently not yet even made the decision to follow the God of his father and grandfather. Yet somehow Jacob understood that if he served God, he would be expected to give Him a tenth of everything he had. Either God had communicated to Jacob directly about tithing or each generation taught tithing to younger generations. This held true for me as a child and later as a father.

"You Can't Out-Give God"

I recall an incident when giving deeply impacted our older son, Joel.

He and our other children learned from Jerusha and me that giving a tenth to God seems to be the biblical starting point for giving. They had often heard us say, "You can always give more, but you shouldn't give less." As far as we know, they applied that principle to their monthly allowance, babysitting money, newspaper route, or any other source of income. Learning this discipline during childhood is easier before both age and income increase.

In the summer between Joel's freshman and sophomore college years, he landed his first high-paying job. He worked the night shift loading trucks for a local food distributor where every dollar he earned was well deserved. When he brought home his first two-week paycheck, the payroll deductions shocked him. The government had taken 20 percent of his hard-earned money in taxes. Suddenly his $1,100 paycheck shrank to $880. My words of "welcome to the working world" did little to comfort his tortured soul.

But Joel knew he wasn't finished. Not only did he still want to give God at least a tenth, but he was faced with the age-old question: "Do I tithe on the gross amount or on the net?" He decided that since God had given him the gross, he should give back to God accordingly and wrote a check for $110. His original $1,100 had now shrunk to $770. Admittedly, it is discouraging for a college student who faces thousands of dollars in tuition fees to see his first paycheck evaporate like drops of water on a hot griddle. Nonetheless, he did what he believed was right.

The following Sunday after the morning service, we checked our church mail slot. Among the assortment of prayer letters and announcements lay an envelope with Joel's name on it.

Shortly after getting home, I walked past his room and noticed him sitting on his bed obviously lost in thought. I decided to go in and ask him what he was thinking about. Almost immediately Joel's eyes welled up with tears, but they were not tears of sorrow.

"God is just so good to me," he said. "Last week when I wrote my check for $110 to the church, it was really hard because I felt like I needed that money for school. Then God gives me this." Joel held the envelope from the church mailbox and removed a check from a family friend. This friend had moved away a year earlier and had felt impressed to send Joel a gift to help with his college costs: $150. "It's just like you say, Dad," he said, smiling through his tears. "You can't out-give God."

Long before God put it in writing, Adam, Eve, Cain, Abel, Abraham, Isaac, and Jacob all knew His will for giving a tithe—one-tenth of all they owned. How did they know? God had told them. This truth then passed from generation to generation until its ultimate communication by God to Moses and its preservation in the Old Testament Law. ■

Growing Outside the Box

"Be doers of the Word, and not hearers only" (James 1:22).

1. As stated near the beginning of this chapter, "the first recorded fight in history was sparked by the issue of giving and ended in murder." If giving back to God is such a good thing, why does it seem to be such a contentious issue?
2. God's interest and pleasure in what we offer to Him is intriguing. As He leans in to observe your giving habits, what do you hope He sees?
3. How do Jesus's words in Matthew 6:24 help explain the conflicts that often arise from money matters?
4. If you have not yet put into practice the principle of tithing (giving 10 percent of your income back to God), what are the greatest obstacles or objections to doing so?
5. Read Malachi 1:6–14 and reflect on the following questions in preparation for the next chapter:
    - What conflict did Malachi describe?
    - How would you describe the attitude of Malachi's audience toward giving to God?
    - How would you describe God's response to their lackluster attitude?

5 FIGHTING WORDS

Thousands of years after Cain killed his brother over a giving matter, people were still waging war over money. Not only do the Old Testament Scriptures begin with money wars in Genesis, the first book, they end the same way in Malachi, the last book.

Malachi's message, short but not sweet, formed a scathing rebuke to people who chose the way of Cain by short-changing God in tithes and offerings. Malachi's message also challenged God's people to return to His original plan for giving—a plan that had not only been spoken to Adam and his descendants, but one that had been written by Moses in the book of Leviticus for all future generations to see.

God Doesn't Have a Plan B

Leviticus is all about what to give to God and how. Not all the offerings had to do with atoning for sin. Of the five primary kinds of offerings, only two of them qualified as atonement for sin. The others served as expressions of fellowship, faith, thanksgiving, and devotion. Some Bible scholars have observed that when all the tithes and offerings prescribed for the care of the Levites, the temple, the festivals, and the poor were put together, the annual giving of a Law-abiding Israelite was about 23 percent.

Without wading through all the different instructions regarding these gifts of worship, we find near the end of the book a summary of God's requirements for the tithe.

> "A tithe of everything from the land, whether grain from the soil or fruit from the trees, belongs to the LORD.... Every tithe of the herd and flock—every tenth animal that passes under the shepherd's rod—will be holy to the LORD" (Leviticus 27:30, 32).

In other words, all of the increase of one's livelihood, whether it came from the land, the crops it produced, or the animals raised on it, qualified as tithable.

This tithe supported the temple worship and the Levites who ministered there. God clearly stated, "I give to the Levites all the tithes in Israel as their inheritance in return for the work they do while serving at the tent of meeting" (Numbers 18:21). No one in all of Israel had an exemption from this—not even the Levites themselves. "Speak to the Levites and say to them: 'When you receive from the Israelites the tithe I give you as your inheritance, you must present a tenth of that tithe as the LORD's offering'" (v. 26).

God was not merely making a suggestion. As far as He was concerned, it was a done deal. The tithe was not even theirs to give or not give. God said, "It belongs to *the Lord*" (Leviticus 27:30, emphasis mine). As to the giving of it, He said, "I give to the Levites all the tithes in Israel" (Numbers 18:21a). Giving was not optional, nor did God have a back-up plan if His people didn't obey.

And if someone didn't give their tithe as prescribed by God, it was clearly not okay. From Cain to Malachi, God expressed His displeasure toward those who refused to worship Him through the giving of a tenth of all their increase. In the case of Malachi's message, God's words could not have been any harsher.

Malachi's Challenge

Malachi wrote his message to a spiritually apathetic Jewish remnant that was simply going through the motions in their relationship with God. They were back in their homeland after seventy years of captivity in Babylon. Their temple had been rebuilt. The walls of their capital had been raised from the rubble. But their spiritual fervor was in ruins. Observing the unbelieving peoples around them, they had noticed that bad people seemed to be prospering more than they were. They thus concluded that following God's guidelines didn't pay.

A marked decline in their sacrifices and offerings to God was symptomatic of their ho-hum attitude. Bringing God their best, first-born animals had become a real drag. "It's such a burden," they might have said with a sigh as they headed for the temple. "What a waste to take such a perfect animal and give it to the priest." Soon they had concluded that any old animal was good enough for God, and it wasn't long until they were offering the worst instead of the best.

Not only were they cutting corners in their animal sacrifices, they were doing the same in other areas. The tithe seemed like a lot to give toward something their heart was not really into, so they started keeping some of it back.

God was not impressed and minced no words in describing their behavior, as recorded in Malachi:

> "'When you bring injured, lame or diseased animals and offer them as sacrifices, should I accept them from your hands?' says the LORD. 'Cursed is the cheat who has an acceptable male in his flock and vows to give it, but then sacrifices a blemished animal to the Lord'" (1:13–14).

If it wasn't enough to call them cheaters and curse them, God added another scathing rebuke.

> "Will a mere mortal rob God?" He asked. "Yet you rob me. But you ask, 'How are we robbing you?' In tithes and offerings. You are under a curse—your whole nation—because you are robbing me" (3:8–9).

Would You Swindle the President?

Imagine the fallout in the church today if the pastor stood before his congregation on Sunday morning and called them a bunch of swindlers and thieves. If he made it out the front door of the church alive, he'd never get back in the following Sunday. Yet those are the very terms God used to describe His covenant people who held back what He said was His rightful due as "a great king" (1:14). Those who kept back their firstborn animals, He called "cheats" or "swindlers," and those who withheld other portions of the tithe, He called "robbers."

In an attempt to help His audience comprehend just how odious their behavior was, God refers to their offering of blind and crippled animals, and suggested, "Try offering them to your governor! Would he be pleased with you? Would he accept you?" (v. 8).

If you were to receive an invitation to the birthday party of a foreign dignitary, what would you choose for a gift? Would you reason that she didn't need anything and go empty handed? How about giving her a dog-eared paperback you didn't want anymore? Do you think she would be impressed? No, even if she didn't need your gift, you would still give one, and I know it would be nice.

How about swindling the federal government out of taxes you owed? What do you think the Internal Revenue Service would say? As I mentioned earlier, income tax time is usually one of my favorite times of year because of my tax refund. A couple of years ago, however, because of some unexpected income God had provided through a particular investment, I found myself owing additional taxes. To be honest, I didn't want to pay them. Why should I give them part of my investment income when they had already taken some 20 percent of my earned income that year? In my opinion, they didn't deserve it.

So why didn't I just fill out my income tax return, and send it in without the check? Why didn't I just tell the IRS I had decided not to give them any more money that year? Would they have been pleased with me? Not at all. The federal government would have slapped me with a stiff penalty for overdue taxes and, if I had persisted in my refusal to pay, they would have charged me with income tax evasion, hauled me into court, and sent me to prison.

Offended Over Money

Malachi's point is impossible to miss: If people would not dare to insult the local governor by giving him their cast-offs, under what pretext did they think they could treat God that way? God was so offended by their insulting thievery that He called down curses on them, reminding them He was not some two-bit governor but the King of the universe: "'I am a great king,' says the LORD

Almighty, 'and my name is to be feared among the nations'" (1:14).

It is not uncommon today for churchgoing people to become defensive when faced with the biblical teaching about giving. The subject is so sensitive that some pastors won't even touch it for fear of offending their congregants. But who should really be offended here? According to Malachi, it is God. To withhold what He had clearly said was His due was so offensive to Him that He was justified in calling His own people swindlers, cheats, and thieves, and invoking upon them the curses of the covenant.

From Cain to Malachi, the issue of giving back to God as an act of worship proved to be contentious. All who knew the Creator God clearly understood that a tithe back to God of all their increase was an expected part of worship. To those like Abel who obeyed His instruction, God expressed His pleasure. To those who didn't, however, God did not simply shrug His shoulders and sigh. He expressed His displeasure in no uncertain terms, calling them to obedience and warning of serious consequences if they didn't.

The Old Testament record began and ended on a rather sour note, provoked by the contentious issue of giving. One might hope the New Testament would tell a different story. With the introduction of grace and the requirements of the Law being fulfilled in the gift of the perfect Lamb of God, maybe giving would become more of a voluntary act of love. Does the freedom of grace eliminate the Old Testament requirement of a tithe or, at the very least, alleviate the contentiousness of the issue? Let's take a look. ■

Growing Outside the Box

"Be doers of the Word, and not hearers only" (James 1:22).

1. God, who is entirely self-sufficient, has no need of anything we might give to Him. Why then do you think He became so animated over the Israelites' lackluster attitude in their offerings?
2. Malachi sought to illustrate the offensiveness of Israel's sub-standard offerings to God by contrasting it to what they would offer a human authority. How does what we give to God compare with what we give to other priorities in our lives—family, friends, hobbies, leisure, etc.—and what might that reveal about our attitude toward God?
3. What words would God use to describe you as a giver?
4. Read Luke 19:1–10 and reflect on the following questions in preparation for the next chapter:
    - How does the description of the rich man in Luke 19:1–10 compare with the rich man described in Luke 18:18–23?
    - What was there in this interaction that would have caused Jesus to declare that Zacchaeus had experienced salvation?
    - What amazes you most about Zacchaeus's transformation, described in Luke 19:8?

PART 2

GRACE GIVING: FREE TO GIVE MORE OR FREE TO NOT GIVE?

The Freedom of Giving in the Age of Grace

6 RAISING THE BAR ON GENEROSITY

Jesus had more to say about money than about any other subject. Randy Alcorn, noted author and advocate of generous giving, observed: "Fifteen percent of everything Christ said relates to this topic—more than his teachings on heaven and hell combined."[7] In the Gospel of Luke, one out of every six verses addresses material things. But lest we think Jesus's gracious words and ways took the edge off this touchy subject, we should note that His teaching often offended His listeners.

In one instance, a wealthy man came to inquire about the requirements for gaining eternal life. Jesus replied: "Sell everything you have and give to the poor, and you will have treasure in heaven" (Luke 18:22). This did not impress the young man. In fact, Jesus's answer so discouraged him that he chose not to follow Him because of what it would cost. Jesus's words to this man seem severe. If He had simply suggested giving a tenth of his riches to the poor, the man might have stayed around. It is almost certain that he was already tithing, for he affirms he had been keeping all the commandments from his youth up.

Why then would Jesus tell a man who was already tithing that he now had to give everything away? Why did Jesus raise the bar so high? Such radical discipleship makes us as western believers squirm. Surely God would not make such a demand of all those who follow Him, would He?

The common explanation is that Jesus knew that the man's money was a hindrance to his faith. By asking him to give everything away, Jesus revealed the man's misplaced allegiance. Certainly, there is some truth to this assertion; otherwise, the man would not have walked away.

Let us not miss the obvious truth communicated through this incident. Jesus was not lowering the bar when it came to giving. He was raising it.

What are the implications for us today? If Jesus would call a Law-abiding, tithing, Old Testament Jew to a higher standard with reference to his money, what might He say to New Testament believers?

The matter of giving back to God does not go away with the dawning of the age of grace. The sheer number of times Jesus chose to address this subject would indicate that, more than ever, money would play a central role in a believer's relationship to God. Time and time again, Jesus stated clearly that unless a person's money was handled properly, it would become a primary hindrance to spiritual life. "You cannot serve God and money" was a common refrain in His teaching (Matthew 6:24, ESV). How then was a believer to handle material things in relation to God?

The Little Man with the Big Wallet

Not all who heard what Jesus had to say about money had such negative reactions. Anyone who has ever attended Sunday School as a child knows the name Zacchaeus. His is one of those stories that, along with David and Goliath, always seemed to make it into the curriculum.

Zacchaeus is best known for the smallness of his stature. But what was truly amazing about him was the greatness of his faith.

Luke, the only Gospel writer to record this incident, chose to focus on three details in his initial description of

Zacchaeus. First, Zacchaeus was a tax collector (Luke 19:2). This fact immediately made him a marked man in Jewish society. The hated occupying forces of Rome imposed heavy taxes. Those tasked with collecting those taxes were deemed collaborators with the enemy. While this stigma was enough to keep most self-respecting Jews from taking the job, there were some, like Zacchaeus, who endured the reproach in return for the financial benefits. One of the perks was that Rome permitted tax collectors to gouge people for more than the amount assessed as long as Caesar got his part. Consequently, tax collectors were not only seen as collaborators, they were also regarded as cheats.

Note that Zacchaeus was not just a tax collector. Luke pointed out that he was the *chief* tax collector. Obviously, he didn't gain his position because of a higher moral standard. When it comes to the world of corruption, it's often the scum that rises to the top. Zacchaeus was probably one of the most despised men in town.

Second, Luke mentioned Zacchaeus's wealth—"He was a chief tax collector and was wealthy" (v. 2). This is the second rich man to be mentioned by Luke in as many chapters. It's obvious he wanted his readers to note the contrast between these two men. One was respected; the other was despised. One followed the Law of God; the other collaborated with the laws of Rome. One was the cream of the crop; the other was the scum of the earth.

Third, Luke mentions Zacchaeus's size—"he was short" (v. 3). Had he been a respected member of society, regardless of his size he would have been able to get to the front of the crowd to see Jesus. The fact that he had to run ahead of the crowd and climb a tree to get a glimpse of Jesus is testimony to how little respect he had among his own people.

Zacchaeus's actions also bore testimony to his spiritual interest. Public gatherings were not a great choice for men of his reputation. This corrupt little collaborator with the bulging billfold was not likely to find a warm reception in the streets of the city. But he braved the crowds because he wanted to see Jesus. What's more, Jesus wanted to see him. When Christ came to the place where Zacchaeus sat, perched high in the tree, He stopped and invited Himself to Zacchaeus's place for a personal visit.

Luke did not write the details of how the visit unfolded, but he does let us in on the conclusion. Touched by his encounter with the Lord, Zacchaeus had a faith experience, which, according to Jesus, resulted in salvation: "Today salvation has come to this house, because this man, too, is a son of Abraham" (Luke 19:9).

What led Jesus to make this declaration? One could conclude that it was simply Jesus's ability to know the human heart that allowed Him to discern the genuineness of Zacchaeus's faith. Yet Luke mentions something else that demonstrated the authentic transformation of this despised little man. It had to do with his money. Zacchaeus made this astounding declaration: "Look, Lord! Here and now I give half of my possessions to the poor, and if I have cheated anybody out of anything, I will pay back four times the amount" (Luke 19:8).

To understand the implications of what he said, let's suppose Zacchaeus had a net worth of $1 million in today's currency. What happened to all his money after he came to faith in Jesus?

First, Zacchaeus made a commitment to give half of it to the poor. Where did he get that idea? Either Jesus talked to him about it or somehow he just knew that investing his resources in this way was the right thing to do. Though this decision would have been viewed as incredibly generous, it still would have left him with a half-million dollars.

But Zacchaeus wasn't finished.

He went on to say that if he had defrauded anyone of anything, he would pay it back—not dollar for dollar, but four to one. This was in keeping with the Old Testament standard of restitution (Exodus 22:1).

We don't know how much of Zacchaeus's wealth was obtained by fraud, but it would not be at all unreasonable to imagine that at least 10 percent of his income may have been fraudulent. This would translate to $100,000 of his total net worth. If he were to repay those he had cheated with a four-to-one payback, it would amount to another payout of $400,000, leaving him with only one-tenth of what he had started with.

Zacchaeus didn't give a tithe; it may be that he only kept a tithe. Zacchaeus gave way outside the box.

This is not a fairy tale. It really happened more than 2,000 years ago to a crooked little rich man turned Christian. Where did he get such notions of generosity? We can only imagine that they came from the teaching and example of the God who had transformed his heart.

A Modern-Day Zacchaeus

While Zacchaeus's transformation is hard for most of us to fathom, his story is not without some modern-day equivalents.

R.G. LeTourneau, whose Caterpillar earth-moving equipment is known and used around the world, started his career in relative obscurity in Stockton, California, where his first job was moving dirt to level out farmland. Between his humble beginnings in 1922 and the onset of World War II seventeen years later, LeTourneau succeeded in building a company so prosperous that it produced 70 percent of all the Army's earth-moving equipment.[8]

Yet more notable than the impact of his business was the impact of his faith. LeTourneau was a man who had learned the grace of generous giving to such an extent that he gave 90 percent of his profits to support kingdom work, keeping just 10 percent for himself. He claimed money came in faster than he could give it away and was thoroughly convinced he could not out-give God. "I shovel it out," he would say, "and God shovels it back, but God has a bigger shovel."[9]

Much like ancient Zacchaeus, LeTourneau seemed to understand the New Testament teaching and example of Christ that grace moves us to give more, not less. Far from abandoning the Old Testament teaching of tithing, Jesus demonstrated that grace takes us beyond it. Yet much of what He had to say was so radical that His detractors mocked Him for it and would-be followers turned away from Him.

If I Were That Wealthy...

A few years ago, I was speaking to a small group of believers in France about the importance of growing in the grace of giving. I had just mentioned the example of R.G. LeTourneau as one who had learned that lesson when a young woman piped up rather defensively, "Well, if I had that much money, I could give 90 percent too!"

While that sentiment seems logical, the only biblical evidence of it happening without a history of giving is that of Zacchaeus. The reality is that the wealthier people are, the less they give as a percentage of their income. Virtually every study on giving patterns in the West has borne this out. Recent analysis of more than 1,000 British donors who had given to charities revealed that those with the lowest incomes gave an average of 4.5 percent to good causes while those earning the most gave just over 2 percent. In the U.S., research has shown that the wealthiest Americans give an average of 1.3 percent of their income while the poorest give 3.2 percent[10]—more than twice as much as their rich counterparts.

For most people there are only two ways to become a generous giver: by radical spiritual transformation of the heart like Zacchaeus, or by starting with whatever you have like LeTourneau. Those who wait to have more money before raising the bar on their giving rarely do.

A Line in the Sand

When it comes to the matter of grace and giving, some see tithing as the proverbial line in the sand. Those like the Pharisees who lived by the letter of the Law saw that line as the place where giving stopped. They believed that Jesus, having abandoned sound reason, was worthy only of derision. But then there were those like Zacchaeus who understood the line in the sand was not the finish line of giving, but a great starting point. ■

Growing Outside the Box

"Be doers of the Word, and not hearers only" (James 1:22).

1. Why do you think money was such an important issue when it came to how Jesus interacted with people?
2. Why do you think the topic of money is so seldom mentioned in many churches today if it is so important to God?
3. In what ways has your encounter with Jesus impacted your response toward those who are poor? How might God want you to deepen your engagement?
4. Read Acts 4:36–5:11 and reflect on the following questions in preparation for the next chapter:
    - What did you learn about generous giving from this story?
    - What do you think sparked these new believers to engage in such radical giving?
    - How does this story seem to raise the bar on generous giving?

7 TAKING OFF THE TRAINING WHEELS

When Joel, our first child, was three years old, we bought him his first bicycle. It was a bright red one, complete with horn, plastic basket on the handlebars, and adjustable training wheels. The training wheels allowed him to ride the bike without tipping over. As he slowly developed his riding skills, we would raise the training wheels a notch at a time so he could learn to balance the bike without the aid of the extra wheels.

The day finally came when Joel began to see the training wheels as restrictive. Rather than helping his progress, they seemed to slow him down. He wanted them removed. It was a triumphant day when he rode his little bike down the paved driveway in front of the house, free of the extra wheels that had formerly kept him upright.

But what did it mean to be free? He was now free to fall, but that was certainly not the desired goal. His freedom from the guiding influence of the training wheels was a liberating freedom that allowed him to do far more than he could prior to their removal. He could now ride faster and maneuver more freely, leaning into corners and turning without the obstruction of those little wheels that had previously held him in a rigid upright position.

Giving 10 percent of our income back to God serves a similar purpose. "Tithing," wrote Randy Alcorn, "isn't the ceiling of giving; it's the floor. It's not the finish line of giving; it's just the starting blocks. Tithes can be the training wheels to launch us into the mindset, skills, and habits of grace giving."[11]

When I was a child, that little red box above the stove served as my training wheels. I doubt I would have ever learned to give outside the box had I never learned to give what was inside the box. I am eternally grateful for those training wheels. I'm also grateful I've moved beyond them.

The regulating influence of the Old Testament Law concerning tithing and a host of other behaviors acted in much the same way as those training wheels. The apostle

Paul likened them to a tutor or schoolmaster who guides a child's progress until he reaches maturity. The removal of the training wheels does not eliminate the need to live according to the principles learned while under their influence. Instead, it enhances our ability to not only live by them, but to surpass them. Those who understood this truth were freed to soar to greater heights. Those who didn't sometimes crashed with sobering consequences.

Money Wars in the Church

The story of Cain and Abel was only the beginning of the money wars that have since characterized human history. Not only was the issue of giving at the root of the first murder in human history, it was also at the heart of the first two deaths in the fledgling New Testament church.

The closing verses of Acts 4 introduced us to a man who, like a child without training wheels, had discovered the freedom of grace giving. His name was Joseph, but he was such a delightful person to be around, he was given the nickname Barnabas, meaning "son of encouragement" (Acts 4:36).

According to the text, Barnabas decided, of his own free will, to sell a field so he could give the proceeds to the ministry of the church. We might liken him to Abel, who freely brought to God the best of what he had. Barnabas's gift to the church seemed outrageously generous. Whereas the Old Testament required God's people to give a tithe of the land, Barnabas gave the land.

What's more, he wasn't alone. Just before the author mentioned Barnabas, he said this about the believers in general: "There was not a needy person among them, for as many as were owners of lands or houses sold them and brought the proceeds of what was sold and laid it at the apostles' feet" (Acts 4:34–35a, ESV). This was one generous group of people! They had obviously thrown off their Old Testament training wheels and were flying along the new highway of grace.

If Barnabas was the New Testament equivalent of Abel, he apparently had his Cain counterpart in a couple named Ananias and Sapphira. Their story is in Acts 5:1–11. Seeing Barnabas's example, they too decided to sell a piece of property. Perhaps they felt the pressure of trying to measure up to the generosity of beloved Barnabas and others like him. They had obviously fallen prey to the comparison game, one that is easy to play but impossible to win. To play the game and come up short leads to discouragement. To play it and come out ahead results in pride. Comparing ourselves with others has never produced a single piece of good fruit. In the case of Ananias and his wife, the fruit was not just bad, it was deadly.

Winning at All Costs

Jerusha likes to play games for the simple pleasure of playing. Why bother tracking points? For a competitive person like me, this is utter nonsense. When the two of us sit down to a game of Scrabble, she'll usually announce that she's not keeping score. This, of course, drives me crazy. Her goal is simply to spell long or unusual words, regardless of their point value. My goal is to get the most points I can. Period. I don't care if she doesn't like my words. In my book, playing ox or axe on a triple word score is far superior to playing some exotic word like oxymoron with no bonus. The goal is to get lots of points, not to spell interesting words.

But in the age-old game of comparison, the only way to play is how Ananias and Sapphira did: to win. Winning is everything, even if it means cheating. And that's exactly what they did.

Having sold their property, they agreed together to give only a portion of the proceeds to the church, but to present their gift as if it represented the full sale price.

The sin that cost this couple their lives was not that they gave less than the full price of the land to the church. The fact is they could have decided not to sell the property at all, or to sell it and give one tenth, or however much they chose. But they knew they couldn't win the comparison game that way. If they sold it and gave only half the proceeds to the church, they feared they would not look good next to "Mr. Generous." But if they gave all the proceeds, then they wouldn't have any left for themselves. The only solution they could think of was to cheat—to misrepresent their gift so as to appear equally generous as beloved Barnabas.

How much should this couple have given? If they had given all of it, they would not have died, for they would have had nothing to lie about. If they had given a tenth like a good Old Testament saint and had not misrepresented the truth, they would not have died either. But what if they had given nothing? What if they had kept the property? What would God have said about that?

Grace Without Boundaries

Perhaps one of the most disconcerting things about grace, especially for those like me who appreciate the security of rules and checklists, is the absence of clearly defined boundaries.

When I was growing up, the church tended to have more boundaries. Some would call it legalism. Others saw it as a simple matter of right and wrong. There was the hair boundary which, for boys, stopped at the top of the ear and the collar. There was the entertainment boundary which often ruled out the possibility of seeing a movie at a theatre. And of course, there was the beverage boundary which made alcohol of any kind and in any amount out of the question.

Today, forty years later, many believers find those ancient boundaries amusing. I know pastors who sport ponytails and missionary men who wear an earring. Years ago, they would have been branded hippies and heretics. Today we say they're in touch with the culture. The "no theatre" boundary has long since disappeared for all but the staunchest opponents of Hollywood even though theatre fare is far worse today than it ever was. What's more, not only do Christians go to theatres, they even rent them to be used as places of worship. Similarly, the question of alcohol has become for many a non-issue.

Boundaryless faith scares me, not because I'm afraid of what I might do but because it makes it hard to keep score. I will allow myself and my family to watch movies, but I still like a boundary. For me it's the ratings. Somewhat arbitrarily, the line I drew as our children were growing up was PG. Even a good war movie won't fit into that category, so from time to time I'd move the boundary. But it made me feel uncomfortable. What if my kids think the boundary is now PG-13, and they don't exercise discernment? When Mel Gibson's movie *The Passion of the Christ* came along with an R rating, I was in a real quandary.

When it comes to giving, boundaryless grace also scares me. I'd like to say Ananias and Sapphira were wrong, not just for lying but for giving half-heartedly. I would like to say that, under grace, they should have given at least 20 percent of their wealth. I would like to tell everyone who reads this book that, under grace, God expects a whole lot more than the tithe. But that's the problem with grace: it does not submit itself to rules. How much should Ananias and Sapphira have given in the age of grace? The answer to that question is as troubling as it is liberating. ■

Growing Outside the Box

"Be doers of the Word, and not hearers only" (James 1:22).

1. In what ways can growing in our giving capacity be freeing?
2. Think about the early believers' process of leaving Judaism and coming to faith in Christ. How did that turn them into such generous givers?
3. If New Testament grace giving is more about freedom to give than it is about meeting the requirements of the Law, how do we decide how much to give?
4. Read 2 Corinthians 9:6–11 in preparation for the next chapter and reflect on what it says about the relationship between freedom and generosity.
5. If you have a bit more time, read 2 Corinthians 8:1–15 and 9:1–11. How can a deeper understanding of grace impact our desire to give?

8 GIVING UNTIL IT FEELS GOOD

Though I have grown significantly in my journey toward generous giving, I have discovered my generosity can be compartmentalized. I can be generous in one area of my life while being miserly in another.

When Crossworld's international staff pass through our home office, Jerusha and I often invite them to our home. For the most part, it is a rewarding experience. My wife never seems to tire of having people around. Entertaining guests energizes her. I, on the other hand, have my limits. When I reach them, my generosity can be quickly engulfed in a cloud of stinginess.

On one occasion, we had been hosting a family in our finished basement for a stretch of several days. Because they were not staying for long, my wife had decided to have them eat most of their meals, except for breakfast, with us. On Saturday morning, I rose early to enjoy some quiet, leisurely time with a cup of coffee and the morning paper. As a special treat for my wife and kids, I decided to sneak out and buy a dozen doughnuts for them to enjoy with breakfast when they woke up. Just as I was heading out the door, my wife crept out of our bedroom and asked where I was going and I told her.

"Maybe you should buy some for our guests, too. We shouldn't have doughnuts without getting some for them."

Unexpectedly my selfish nature bristled to the surface.

"Why shouldn't we?" I asked. "Why do we have to provide every meal for them? They have food in their fridge. Let them get their own breakfast."

I lost the debate and trudged off to the doughnut shop, grumbling all the way there and back about the extra few dollars I was obliged to spend on doughnuts. Upon my return, I went downstairs and put the doughnuts by our guests' door to surprise them when they got up. I finally started feeling a little better about my forced generosity, imagining to myself how grateful they would be to awake to fresh doughnuts, and how they would surely come bounding up the stairs to shower me with praise for my unspeakable kindness.

Much to my dismay, breakfast came and went, and the day moved on without any word about the doughnuts. My selfish musings returned. So that's all the thanks I get for walking all the way to the doughnut store on a Saturday morning while everyone else sleeps, and spending my hard-earned money on doughnuts that people don't even appreciate.

How Many Doughnuts?

So, how many doughnuts should I have bought that Saturday morning? If God had been in on my conversation with Jerusha that day, I kind of think He would have taken my side and said, "Dale, buy a dozen for your family and let your guests fend for themselves." Why? Because God loves cheerful givers. God is not interested in our giving when it comes from a stingy heart.

He said as much to Ananias and Sapphira when Peter confronted them about their deception: "While it (your land) remained unsold, did it not remain your own? And after it was sold, was it not at your disposal?" (Acts 5:4, ESV). Peter's point was clear: it was their land to do with it as they pleased. No one made them sell it. And no one made them give any of the proceeds to the church. God would have preferred them to have kept their land rather than to have given it grudgingly. In light of their attitude, Ananias and Sapphira should have given nothing.

Enough to Make One Sick

I'm glad our missionary guests didn't know how selfish I was with my miserable doughnuts that infamous Saturday morning. If they had, they probably wouldn't have eaten them. Stingy giving makes the receiver sick. The writer of Proverbs warned his readers:

> Do not eat the food of a begrudging host, do not crave his delicacies; for he is the kind of person who is always thinking about the cost. 'Eat and drink,' he says to you, but his heart is not with you. You will vomit up the little you have eaten and will have wasted your compliments (23:6–8).

I would rather have bread and water offered to me by someone who wants me at his table than steak and shrimp from someone who doesn't. Notice that what determines the appropriateness of a gift is not what someone says, but what they think in their heart. Graciously offered gruel tastes a whole lot better than stingily offered steak.

Who God Really Loves

Although one of God's foremost characteristics is love, there are surprisingly few statements in Scripture where the object of His love is stated in detailed terms. The best known would be the declaration of the apostle in John 3:16, "For God so loved *the world*...." (emphasis mine). God loves the world of lost people. He also loves His own children: "God so loved us" (1 John 4:11). But one of the rarest and most specific statements about the object of His love is found in 2 Corinthians 9:7. There, the apostle Paul wrote, "God loves a cheerful giver." His meaning is made crystal clear by the words prefacing that statement: "Each of you should give what you have decided in your heart to give, not reluctantly or under compulsion, for God loves a cheerful giver."

Cheerful givers gladly give from their heart. They don't give to match the generosity of others, or because they know it's expected. They give because their heart is so full of gratitude and joy that they can't hold it back. Biblical giving—giving with the Old Testament training wheels removed—grace-giving if you will, is not about how much you have to give, but about how much you want to give.

The English word *cheerful* is translated from the Greek word *hilaros*. Does that sound familiar? It gives us our

English word *hilarious.* It is an intriguing way for God to describe givers who are the special object of His affection.

In the world of humor, something that's *hilarious* doesn't merely makes you smile. It is not even something that makes you laugh. It is something that makes you laugh so hard you cry. It's not forced. It's not fabricated. It's not done in measured, controlled installments. Rather, it is something so funny that it bursts forth in unrestrained, side-splitting fits of laughter that cause your eyes to overflow with tears.

Imagine giving on that scale! Not forced or fabricated. Not measured or programmed. But pure, unrestrained, joy-driven, heartfelt giving. That's the kind of giving God longs to see bursting forth from His people. That's the kind of giving that has little to do with percentages and everything to do with passion.

The Worship of Laughter

Pastor and author Chuck Swindoll painted a delightful picture of what it might look like in a church service on Sunday morning if God's people were seized with this kind of giving.

> I have never been able to understand why everyone in the church looks so serious during the offering. Wouldn't it be great if when the offering plates were passed in church next Sunday that instead of grim looks, stoic silence, and soft organ music you heard laughter? I can just imagine: "Can you believe we're doing this? Put it in the plate, honey. Isn't this great? Put it in!"... followed by little ripples of laughter and applause across the place of worship. Wonderful! Why not? Deep within the heart there is an absence of any compulsion, only spontaneous laughter.[12]

When was the last time you experienced worship like that? When was the last time you could hardly wait for the offering plate to be passed so you could joyfully worship God? If you have a hard time imagining such worship, try reading 1 Chronicles 29. It describes when David and his people gave of their wealth to build the temple—the most generous and joyful worship experience recorded in Scripture. Make sure you notice how it ends. Prostrate before God. That's right. They were so moved by worshipping God through giving, that they fell on their faces. When was the last time you saw any group of people prostrate before God—especially in response to a giving experience?

What if we were to discover the sheer, unrestrained joy of giving? What if we found it every bit as delightful as the most hilarious evening of laughter we have ever known? It would forever put to rest the question of whether a tithe was the right standard of giving, and we would long for the next outburst of hilarious generosity to seize our hearts. ■

Growing Outside the Box

"Be doers of the Word, and not hearers only" (James 1:22).

1. Think about your heart attitude when it comes to giving. On a scale where one represents "grudgingly" and ten represents "joyfully," where would you put yourself? Why?
2. What needs to change in your own heart for you to move more toward joyful giving?
3. Take time to read the story of joy-filled giving recorded in 1 Chronicles 29 and record what you learn from it about generous giving.
4. Do something generous for someone this week—your pastor, a co-worker, your spouse, an underfunded ministry you're aware of—and note what the experience was like.

9 WHEN YOU CAN'T AFFORD TO GIVE

It's easy to say that generosity can be as enjoyable as side-splitting laughter, but if this is true, why aren't more people eager to give? Perhaps it's because joyful giving does not mean painless giving. Generosity is also costly. Every choice to give means making a conscious choice to keep less for myself. That may mean fewer meals eaten out, fewer square feet in my dream house, or less frequent replacement of my car for a newer model. In some cases, it may even mean less of what I may legitimately need. If you're like many people, you probably don't have a lot of extra money just waiting to be spent.

So how do you give generously when you feel you can't afford it? Could God possibly want you to be a growing giver if you've lost your job, are trying to put two kids through college, or are saving up for a down payment on your first house?

An Opportunity Too Good to Miss

One of the most powerful stories of God's commitment to provide not only for His servants, but also for those who release their resources to support their fellow servants is found in the story of Elijah and the widow of Zarephath. (1 Kings 17:7–24). You may recall that Elijah had been sent by God to a remote brook in the hill country to be cared for by ravens. Morning and evening they delivered bread and meat to the prophet. Hidden away from the raging King Ahab and his bloodthirsty wife Jezebel, Elijah was well provided for.

But then the brook dried up. Certainly, the God who could command ravens to deliver groceries could have commanded the brook to keep flowing. But He had other plans. He took Elijah from his comfortable, safe haven and sent him to the Gentile region of Sidon where He had commanded a widow to provide for him. That was undoubtedly a stretch for this Jewish prophet. To be sent to a pagan land, to the very birthplace of Baal worship, and have him depend on a Gentile widow for his sustenance would have been highly disagreeable.

I have often wondered how Elijah might have felt about this. One could imagine that it might have been humbling if not outright humiliating. To depend on a widow would have been hard enough, but this was no mere widow. She was a pagan widow, a penniless pagan widow, and a dying, penniless, pagan widow. It would have been humiliating indeed had it not been that God had told Elijah of His plan to bless this woman in response to her giving.

I can just imagine Elijah arriving in town. *Where is she? I can hardly wait to find her. This is going to be so incredible!* He came upon the woman as she was gathering some sticks and called out to her, asking that she fetch him a drink of water. Then, almost as an afterthought he added, "And bring me, please, a piece of bread" (v. 11).

The woman replied, "I don't have any bread—only a handful of flour in a jar and a little olive oil in a jug. I am gathering a few sticks to take home and make a meal for myself and my son, that we may eat it—and die" (v. 12). But Elijah wouldn't take no for an answer and assured her this was an opportunity she couldn't afford to miss.

Humanly speaking, this woman could not afford to give. But from God's perspective, this is exactly what she needed to do. Had she made her decision based on her limited perspective, she would have done exactly what she had said—eaten her last meal and died. Fortunately for her, she took a step of faith and gave what she couldn't afford. The miraculous provision that followed kept her and her son alive for the duration of the famine.

All too often we, like that widow, are tempted to base our giving priorities on what we think we can afford. We'd like to become hilarious givers. We'd like to increase our giving. But the reality is we have bills to pay, a family to feed, a house to maintain… the list is endless. If we give what we need for other necessities, we may find ourselves in an impossible situation. It is precisely for this reason that God sometimes wants us to step out in faith and do it. He loves getting involved in impossible situations.

Giving It Away and Getting It Back

As the leader of a faith-based ministry, I regularly interact with people about the possibility of giving to the ministry of the gospel through our organization. I believe there are some whom God wants to make a commitment, and there are others He doesn't. I don't claim to know God's will for their lives and finances, so I just present them with the opportunity and leave it for them to determine before God.

Several times in my conversations, I have had people say, "We'd like to help, but we just can't afford it right now." Though I understand what they're saying, I can't help but wonder if they're not missing the point. The issue is not whether we can afford to give. The issue is whether God wants us to give. Sometimes those who can least afford it are the ones God is nudging to give anyway so He can demonstrate His ability to provide and bless in ways that grow their faith.

During the summer between Jerusha's junior and senior years of college, she had made a commitment to spend her summer serving in a cross-cultural ministry in Argentina. She raised the required funds for her trip, promising God that, should she have anything left over at the end of her time there, she would give it back to Him. She returned home to San Diego at the end of the summer, just in time for the start of her senior year, with $400 to spare. She considered how nice it would be to put that money toward school supplies and new clothes. After all, she earned no income that summer. Hadn't she selflessly served God all summer in Argentina? Wouldn't she be justified in using this leftover money for such necessities? But she wasn't about to renege on her commitment. She took the money and put it in the offering plate on Sunday morning.

On Jerusha's way out of church that morning, a woman asked if she could speak with her. As it turned out, the woman was in the retail clothing business and owned a women's clothing store that she was closing. She proceeded to explain to Jerusha that she had a whole inventory she needed to get rid of. She invited Jerusha to go to the store that week and choose as many outfits as she would like—at no charge. A few days later Jerusha did so, picking out enough clothes to last her for the entire year.

The value of those clothes and what Jerusha learned about God were worth far more than the $400 she had given away. Some might be tempted to think Jerusha would have still received the gracious offer of free clothes, even if she had kept the $400. If the offer of free clothes was simply coincidence, I suppose I might agree. But giving and receiving is not a matter of human coincidence. It is a matter of divine decree. In Luke 6:38 when Jesus said "Give, and it will be given to you," He was not talking about coincidence. He was talking about God's commitment to release His resources to those who have learned to give—even when they humanly can't afford to. One of the reasons He loves to find generous givers is because He loves to demonstrate His miraculous provision in their lives.

Obedience Sometimes Produces Miraculous Results

There is no logical explanation for how someone could fare better on 70 or 80 or 90 percent of their income than they could by keeping it all for themselves. Yet God's Word and the personal experience of generous Christians down through the centuries have proven that obedience to God can produce miraculous results.

One such example is recorded for us in the story of Israel's deliverance from Egypt. As over 1 million people entered the punishing desert life of the Sinai Peninsula, the nation faced an intensely practical problem: Where would they find food to sustain so many people for weeks and months of desert wandering?

God's miraculous solution was to provide bread from heaven (Exodus 16). Every morning a new supply of heavenly wafers covered the ground like dew, and the Israelites were told to go and gather only as much as they needed for that day. God warned them not to stockpile any for the next day. He wanted them to trust Him for their daily sustenance. Some, however, decided to stock up anyway. We don't mind stale manna. Better to have stale manna than no manna at all—you know, in case the Lord decides not to send fresh stuff tomorrow morning. Whatever the reasoning behind their disobedience, the result was that the leftovers became rotten and wormy. God was not pleased by their lack of faith.

Then God told them that on the sixth day, they should gather enough for two days because He did not want them to work on the Sabbath. This, of course, made no logical sense. If it would rot on a weekday, why would it not rot on a Sabbath weekend? The reason was simple: God wanted them to trust and obey. If they did, He would miraculously provide. Those who obeyed discovered their bread from day six remained untainted on day seven. Those who disobeyed and went out looking for bread on the Sabbath discovered there was none to be found.

An even more astounding example of God's commitment to provide miraculously for those who honor Him with their resources is given to us in His instructions for the Sabbath year and the year of Jubilee. Every seventh year (the Sabbath year), the Israelites were to give their land a complete rest (Leviticus 25:1–7). They were to plant and harvest no crops whatsoever. Every fiftieth year (the year of Jubilee), they were supposed to do the same (25:8–55).

What this meant in practical terms was that once every fifty years, they would have to survive for three full years on a single harvest. Since every seventh year was to be a Sabbath rest year, the forty-ninth year would be a year without planting or harvesting, as would be the fiftieth year of Jubilee. Consequently, the harvest from year forty-eight would need to last them until the harvest of year fifty-one when they were again allowed to work their fields.

How could they possibly hope to survive? How could one year's crop provide for three years of need? The answer was quite simple from God's perspective: "I will send you such a blessing in the sixth year that the land will yield enough for three years" (Leviticus 25:21).

God's Hand-Me-Downs

A few years after our "Frosty-less" walk in Dallas, Jerusha and I landed in San Diego. We had just finished our seminary studies and were preparing to move to France as new cross-cultural workers. As you might imagine, those days between full-time graduate studies and cross-cultural ministry came with very few extras. By God's grace we had graduated with no debt, but we also had no money. Arriving in San Diego, I found work as the clean-up guy in a concrete business. The strong mind and weak back of a full-time student were quickly put to the test. This was not exactly the "ministry" I had envisioned for myself as a seminary graduate, but at least it paid the rent and put a little food on the table.

There was little room in our budget for more than that. In fact, not only were Frosties out of the question, so were new clothes for our one-year-old son. I suppose you could argue that by cutting back on our giving we could have afforded clothes for our growing boy. But to be honest, the thought just never occurred to us. In fact, I hadn't even noticed that our son was outgrowing his clothes. Of course, Jerusha had, but in her contented, trusting way, she decided not to mention it to me. As I found out later, however, she was mentioning it to God.

One day as she prayed about the need, she asked God to lay it on the heart of someone who had older boys to consider passing along some of their used clothes to our son. As she prayed, a certain name popped into her mind: Julie Hogan. Julie was a young mom from the church we had begun attending and she had three boys, all older than our son. Since, however, we were new in the church and virtually unknown by the family in question, Jerusha dismissed it from her mind: Julie didn't even know us.

Two days later while Jerusha worked around the house, the phone rang, and she answered it.

"Hello, Jerusha? I'm not sure if you know me, but my name is Julie Hogan and I'm from the church." I don't know whether Julie even got the rest of the words out of her mouth before my wife's eyes flooded with tears.

"The reason I'm calling," Julie continued, "is because I was just wondering if you might be able to use some clothes my boys have outgrown."

Suddenly my son had more clothes than he could wear, and quality ones at that—much nicer than anything we would have bought new from the store. My wife had told no one about the need, not even her own husband—no one, that is, except the One who loves to open the windows of heaven when He sees one of His trusting children in need. This is one of the reasons God loves "hilarious" givers—those who give until it hurts, who give when they can least afford it. Such giving opens the door for Him to move in miraculous ways. In the case of Jerusha and Julie, it was as if God Himself handed down the hand-me-downs, clothing our son with heavenly garments.

In *The Treasure Principle*, author Randy Alcorn told the story of a couple who were challenged by evangelist Bill Bright to give a million dollars to the cause of the gospel. Of that incident, he wrote:

This amount was laughable to Scott—far beyond anything he could imagine since his machinery business was generating an income of under fifty thousand dollars a year.

Bill asked, "How much did you give last year?" Scott felt pretty good about his answer: "We gave seventeen thousand dollars, about 35 percent of our income."

Without blinking an eye, Bill responded, "Over the next year, why don't you make a goal of giving fifty thousand dollars?"

Scott thought Bill hadn't understood. That was more than he had made all year! But Scott and his wife decided to trust God with Bill's challenge, asking him to do the impossible. God provided in amazing ways… the Lewises were able to give the fifty thousand dollars. The next year they set a goal of giving one hundred thousand dollars. Again, God provided. In 2001 they passed the one-million-dollar mark in their giving.[13]

Does Your Faith Have Any Stretch Marks?

Giving is a painful, joyful experience. Those two adjectives don't seem to go together and yet they do. In some ways, it is a bit like childbirth (I am told). I have never seen my wife in so much pain as when she gave birth to each of our four children. Yet I have never seen her so joyful as when she cradled the outcome of her pain in her arms.

In a similar way, faith giving cannot take place without pain. It is not easy to believe God for a million dollars in giving when you're only at the $17,000 mark. Moreover, such giving requires great sacrifice. To give away what you might legitimately spend on things that would increase your personal security and comfort is painful. Yet faith that is so stretched is rewarded with great joy.

Giving and childbirth also have this in common: both are unbelievably stretching experiences. There is no easy way to give birth to an eight-pound child. The joy is accompanied by much stretching and pain. Becoming a generous giver is not a simple, painless process either. It cannot come without great stretching of your faith. But oh, the joy of not only seeing the results, but also of experiencing God in the process.

When it comes right down to it, this is the kind of giving that truly delights God. Giving that stretches, that hurts—giving that we can ill afford is giving that moves God. ■

Growing Outside the Box

"Be doers of the Word, and not hearers only" (James 1:22).

1. What is your reaction to the idea of giving when you can't afford to do so? What would you say is at the root of that reaction?
2. What have you read in the chapter that motivates you to give when you feel like you can't afford to?
3. What do you think caused the widow to change her mind and respond to Elijah's request?
4. In what way might God want you to "stretch" in your giving journey?

10 AVOIDING UNHEALTHY EXTREMES

In his pursuit of life's meaning, King Solomon wrote a book that many a reader over the centuries has found puzzling. It is an honest look at life's pursuits in the light of eternity. Many readers are familiar with the oft-repeated refrain, "Vanity of vanities! All is vanity" (Ecclesiastes 1:2, ESV). Solomon then catalogued a vast array of human experiences that promise fulfillment but never deliver. Money was one of them, but it was certainly not the only one. Solomon also mentioned alcohol, women, knowledge, power, entertainment, personal accomplishment, and much more.

Perhaps more puzzling than what appears to be a pessimistic, depressing outlook on life is that Solomon included what we would consider to be many wholesome—even righteous—pursuits in the list of experiences that, for him, came up empty. One such example he recorded is, "Do not be overrighteous, neither be overwise—why destroy yourself? Do not be overwicked, and do not be a fool—why die before your time? It is good to grasp the one and not let go of the other" (7:16–18a).

Solomon seemed to suggest it is possible to be too righteous. How can that be? If a little righteousness is good, wouldn't a lot be even better? Then in the next breath, he seemed to recommend moderate wickedness as opposed to being excessively so. How could he recommend moderate righteousness, much less moderate wickedness? The answer seems to lie in the phrase that follows: "Whoever fears God will avoid all extremes" (v. 18b). Solomon was not condoning moderate amounts of wickedness, nor was he suggesting that being a lukewarm follower of God was okay. Rather, he was saying that in all of life, yes, even in righteous behavior, it is possible to go to unhealthy extremes.

A Dangerous Extreme

One of the dangers I have become aware of in my own quest to be increasingly generous is that of being imbalanced when it comes to the objects of my generosity. As I have already indicated, I can be generous in one area of my life while being stingy in another. I can give thousands of dollars to the church and missions, yet begrudge a five-dollar box of doughnuts to my house guests.

Where I have been particularly aware of this danger is in relation to my own family. There have been times over the years that I have shortchanged my wife and children in my zeal to become exceptionally generous to kingdom pursuits. There have been times when I have said yes to other needs at the expense of saying no to my children. I am not saying this is always a bad thing. Far too often in western society we have gone to the other extreme of making little gods out of our children by giving them everything they could possibly want.

What I am talking about here is the opposite extreme. It is the extreme of taking such pride in my giving to the things of God, even though I may never tell anyone what I give, that I end up being cheap with my own family. This is an extreme I am learning to avoid. While I want my children to understand the joy of giving and the sacrifice of denying themselves, I don't want them to have the view of a father who is a cheapskate. If I want them to see God as a generous Father, they need to see me, their earthly father, in that light as well.

Righteous Rip-Off

Among the many rebukes Jesus gave to the hypocritical religious establishment of His day, one had to do with how they were ripping off their own family members in the name of charitable giving. These religious leaders were scrupulous tithers. They not only gave a tenth of their income, they tithed right down to the last bit of seasoning in their spice racks. Jesus said, "You give a tenth of your spices—mint, dill and cumin. But you have neglected the more important matters of the law—justice, mercy and faithfulness" (Matthew 23:23).

One of the areas of their neglect was in relation to their own parents. Jesus pointed out their responsibility to care for their aging parents, which they were ignoring under the pretense of having committed that money to religious causes. "Whatever help you might otherwise have gotten from me," they said to their parents, "is a gift devoted to God" (Matthew 15:5, WEB).

In other words, they were saying to mom and dad: "I'd sure like to be able to help you, but you know I'm a servant of God and I've given my life to the cause. All my money is tied up in kingdom endeavors. Maybe you should give the Social Security Administration a call." Though their so-called righteousness was merely a pretext for neglecting their parents, Jesus communicated an even more basic truth that we must not miss: caring for our families is every bit as spiritual as making contributions to religious endeavors. Generous charitable giving that ignores the fundamental needs of my own family does not please God.

Don't Cheap-Out on Your Family

I'm not saying I was necessarily being negligent in failing to buy new clothes for my growing son. Nor am I suggesting my children have a God-given right to receive a car from mom and dad as a graduation gift. It has been extremely beneficial for our kids to learn the sacrifice of self-denial. They have not adopted the attitude of entitlement embraced by some of today's youth. They have learned the value of hard work and the disciplines of saving and sacrifice. They have learned, I believe, to be content with considerably less than the average North American millennial. Yet, there have been times when, in my zeal to give a little more to "kingdom endeavors," I fear I may have communicated to my own family a cheapness that is not becoming to our heavenly Father of whom we are representatives.

Too Cheap to Buy a Pencil Case

I think of one incident when our son, Joel, was in fourth grade. We were living in France at the time, and the dollar was taking a particularly hard hit on the currency exchange. We didn't have much room in our budget for extras. One day just a few weeks before the start of the school year, Joel came to me with his tattered pencil case in hand and mentioned he would like a new one before the start of school. I looked at him and the old case in his hand before answering.

"I'm sorry, son, but we can't afford to buy a new one right now. But you know what? If God wants you to have a new pencil case, He can provide one. Why don't we ask Him right now?"

As I look back, I can hardly believe I said that, but I did. What's more, I was sincere. We didn't have much money to spare at the time. At the same time, we had not cut back on our giving to the church and missions. In fact, we were giving more than we had ever given. In retrospect, my giving priorities (and perhaps savings priorities) were out of whack. At the time, Jerusha and I were giving nearly a thousand dollars a month to kingdom pursuits, yet I didn't feel like I could afford to buy my child a new pencil case.

Joel and I prayed that day, although I doubt my prayer was offered in faith as much as it was an excuse for my apparent inability to give. Despite it all, God chose to answer. A few days later, the area where we lived was struck by a fierce electrical storm. In the process the lines near our house were hit by lightning and the electrical surge ruined our fax machine. The machine had been given to us by a company whose office was clearing out some of their used equipment. Since I hadn't paid anything for it, I didn't even think about making an insurance claim until a friend suggested I should. I contacted my insurance company, giving them the make and model of the ruined machine, almost sure they would refuse it. To my amazement, they responded almost immediately with a check for 4,000 francs—roughly $800 at the time. Guess what? My son got his pencil case.

I'd like to think God responded to my faith, but I suspect it was more likely another example of His grace to the undeserving. My son needed a pencil case. I knew it and God knew it. I should have bought a pencil case for him and trusted God to provide. At that moment, he needed to see not just a generous God, but a generous father. In the end, he saw the one, and I hope in the long run, that he has also seen the other.

Free to Be Generous to God and People

One of the greatest benefits of learning to give outside the box is that we can develop an enlarged capacity to give when needs arise. While Jerusha and I make it our practice to allocate a certain percentage of our resources to charitable causes, not all of it is committed to a designated cause. What this means is that after our commitment to give a certain amount to our local church and to the missionaries and other organizations we support, we have discretionary funds left over to give wherever we see a need. Consequently, we have rarely felt like we simply had nothing left to give. This has given us great freedom.

When our four children began heading off to university a few years ago, we were suddenly faced with a dilemma. How could we continue to give at the level we had grown to over more than twenty years of marriage, while at the same time help our children with their educational costs? One year of schooling was almost a third of our annual salary. When our second child joined the first at university, the annual cost of educating our children went completely out of sight.

What could we do? As unspiritual as it may sound, we chose to use a portion of our discretionary giving to help our children. The result was that, without reducing our commitments to the local church and missions, we were able to help our children so that, between their academic scholarships, part-time employment, and our financial help, they remained virtually debt-free throughout their university years. Though the total cost of their education came to a staggering $400,000, the combined amount of their school debt when all four had graduated was only $20,000. Though only a fraction of their college funding came from us, we could not have ministered to our children at a time of significant need in their lives if we, as their parents, hadn't grown as givers.

To be honest, we are utterly amazed at how God has provided for and prospered us even in the face of increased financial demands. How is it possible that we, a single-income family, with annual university costs that some years topped $50,000, have been able to maintain our giving commitments, help with educational costs, increase in our overall financial health, and still have room for more discretionary giving? I am thoroughly convinced the answer lies in the multitude of promises God has given in His

Word about His commitment to those who honor Him with their wealth. I do not say that for my own glory as a giver, but to His glory as the Provider.

I Can't Tell You How It Got There

Biblical generosity is not defined by whether we get a tax-deductible receipt for it. It's not just about giving to your local church or favorite missions organization. It's about a lifestyle of treating people—family, friends, co-workers, and even strangers—generously. God loves to bless generosity—regardless of its object.

Phil and Linda are friends of ours whose lives excel in generosity. And they have a multitude of stories illustrating God's favor on those who are generous.

A few years ago, they sensed God putting a desire in their hearts to purchase a second residence—not for themselves, but for the purpose of sharing it with pastors and missionaries as a place to get away and rest.

While away celebrating their anniversary, it came to their attention that a house was for sale. They looked at it and liked it, but for some reason felt it wasn't for them. A few months later, the owner called to say the home had not sold and he had dropped the price. In the intervening time, the desire to do something like this had simply grown stronger in Phil and Linda's hearts, so this time they decided to go ahead and purchase the house. They had enough in their bank account to pay cash for the house and all the furnishings.

Now they owned a second house they planned to share, free of charge, with others, but they had spent down their personal resources with no provision to replenish their reserves. Yet God apparently had a plan. Phil said, "One year later all the money was back in our account—and I can't tell you how it got there. It was a God thing."

Not a Money-Back Guarantee

God's commitment to bless generous givers is not a money-back guarantee or an ironclad pledge of financial prosperity. He does not promise to mysteriously fill your bank account while you're sleeping. God does not promise to let my children, or yours, graduate debt-free. I know many obedient followers of Jesus whose children have college debt, and I am in no way saying it is because they aren't generous givers. If God has chosen to bless us with such provision, it has nothing to do with our financial acumen and everything to do with His choice to be generous to us.

- He is the One who said: "Honor the LORD with your wealth, with the firstfruits of all your crops; then your barns will be filled to overflowing…" (Proverbs 3:9–10a).
- He is the One who said: "Bring the whole tithe into the storehouse… and see if I will not throw open the floodgates of heaven and pour out so much blessing that there will not be room enough to store it" (Malachi 3:10).
- It is God who promised that by our standard of measure it would be measured to us in return (Luke 6:38).
- And it is God who said to those who sow generously that they would also reap generously (2 Corinthians 9:6).

God said all of these. And my family has experienced them. These are not money-back guarantees, but they are general principles which we have found to be true.

Growing Your Giving Muscle

Just before my younger son, Nathan, went off to university a few years ago, he challenged me to an arm wrestle. With all that testosterone flowing through his teenage body, he figured the time had come to give the old guy a run for his money. What he didn't realize is that an old bear can still have a lot of fight in him. As we locked arms, he discovered a little more resistance than anticipated and his youthful confidence began to fade. I retained my title as the undefeated champion that day, but the soreness in my arm lasted for longer than I'd like to admit and reminded me that my days were numbered.

When he graduated from university and came home for the summer, he was not the same young boy of four years earlier. He had changed in many ways, not the least of which was that he had bulked up. Sometime amidst the demanding social and academic rigors of university life, he found time to pump iron. His muscles grew. What he couldn't do before college, he can do today. Not wanting to crush my ego, he has never challenged me to another arm wrestle, but I know beyond a shadow of a doubt that my days as reigning champ are over. Every time I see him in a t-shirt, this old bear feels more and more like a teddy bear—soft, that is.

Though you may not have realized it, you have what could be called a giving muscle. The more you exercise it, the bigger and stronger it gets. The stronger it gets, the greater your capacity for giving. What was previously a challenge gradually becomes easier. And what was formerly impossible becomes achievable. But it doesn't happen overnight. Like bodybuilding, it takes time and effort, and does not come without some pain. But how gratifying it is to see our capacity grow.

The giving muscle is one I long for my children to develop. It will give them power and freedom and confidence in life that will bless them in ways they could never have imagined. They are the reason I chose to write about my experiences with giving in the first place. I wanted them to learn what I am learning. But for them to embrace it, they must see me as their father flexing my giving muscle in my own home by being a generous provider for them. ■

Growing Outside the Box

"Be doers of the Word, and not hearers only" (James 1:22).

1. Would your friends and family describe you as a generous person? Why or why not?
2. In what aspects of life (other than money) does your behavior communicate to others that God is a generous God?
3. In what way may you need to move away from an extreme to a more balanced management of God's resources?
4. What is one thing you could do this week to express God's generosity to a parent, a child, a friend, a co-worker, or even a stranger?

11 THE GENEROSITY KILLER

While the exercise of faith is a major factor in one's quest to grow in their giving, there is another matter of critical importance that must be addressed, particularly in North America, if we ever hope to become exceptional givers. It is the matter of personal debt. Nothing will hinder the development of your giving muscle more than debt. Simply put, you cannot learn to be a growing giver if you do not learn to be a shrinking spender. Furthermore, to address the issue of giving without equal attention to the issue of spending is not only ineffective, it leads to frustration and discouragement. It is like trying to bail water from a sinking boat without first plugging the hole that is letting in water.

Pinned Down Under a Load of Debt

North Americans are among the most prosperous and the most debt-ridden people on earth. Consumer debt in America hit a new record high of $14.3 trillion during the first quarter of 2020.[14] The Federal Reserve reported that in 2019 household debt jumped by $601 billion—the most in 12 years. The average American now has about $38,000 in personal debt, excluding home mortgages.[15] Northwestern Mutual's 2018 Planning and Progress Study reported that 2 in 10 Americans spend between 50 percent and 100 percent of their monthly income on debt repayment.[16]

Between monthly mortgage payments, car payments, and repayment of college and credit card debt, many people have nothing left to give. They are already spending more than they are earning and are slowly sinking deeper into debt. By over-spending, they have dug themselves a pit of unmanageable debt they can't get out of while credit card companies, like willing accomplices, hand them a bigger and bigger shovel to dig with. The Bible likens this predicament to slavery: "The borrower is slave to the lender" (Proverbs 22:7).

To illustrate the danger of getting buried under debt, Bruce Howard, professor of Business and Economics at

Wheaton College, told this story of Jake, a cowboy who met an untimely death in eastern Montana around 1920. Driving a herd of cattle across the open range, Jake's horse stepped in one of the many prairie dog holes that dot the landscape, hurling horse and rider to the ground. The horse died instantly of a broken neck. Jake survived, but found himself pinned under his horse.

Trying unsuccessfully to dig himself out from under the weight of the horse, Jake then used his rope to lasso a nearby rock or tree and winch the horse off him. This too failed. A final effort to free himself from the horse with his jack knife proved equally futile.

With nothing left to do, the cowboy finally resigned himself to the inevitable. No one witnessed his death, but the artifacts preserved in the dusty ground—the rope, the winch, the horse, and the knife—bear witness to his fate.[17]

If the horse represents debt, it would be naïve to suggest we should avoid debt as cowboys should avoid horses. Just as it is inconceivable that a cowboy could manage without a horse, so in our society it is difficult to imagine life without some measure of debt, be it a mortgage on one's house or the convenience of a credit card to facilitate purchases. The point, however, is that debt, like horses, can pose real danger when things get out of control. The same debt that can help you in one circumstance can prove fatal in another.

If you don't get the dead weight of debt off you, it will invariably prove fatal, not only to your ability to become a generous giver, but in many cases to your relationships and your general well-being.

If debt has become a dead weight that has you pinned under its weight, you must at all costs extricate yourself. No other financial decision at this moment is more important than this one. For many who have unsuccessfully struggled to get free, that probably means getting some outside help. Dave Ramsey's Financial Peace University has been instrumental in helping hundreds of thousands of people dig themselves out from debt and begin living lives characterized by freedom and generosity. Look it up at daveramsey.com.

Another valuable resource in this regard is Crown Financial Ministries. Their goal is to help people and communities thrive to the glory of God by applying sound biblical wisdom to the management of our resources. You can find them at crown.org.

Learning to Say No to Consumerism

Inherent to defeating the debilitating power of debt in your life is developing the power to say no to rampant consumer instincts. Our society has taken consumerism to such an extreme that it is virtually impossible to fathom life without spending. The very well-being of our economy is dependent on our commitment to spend.

Shortly after the global financial meltdown that rocked the world in late 2008, the U.S. government rolled out a new economic stimulus plan designed to stave off an economic recession. Those who qualified received a government check in the mail, with a letter encouraging them to go out and spend it. Imagine the logic! "Hard economic times are upon us. Spend, spend, spend!"

So accustomed have we become to spending, that a Saturday is not complete without multiple trips to Walmart, Home Depot, Costco, IKEA, or any of a thousand other stores vying for our dollars. In many cases it has nothing to do with need and everything to do with greed. Far more than meeting need, credit-based buying has become the way to fulfill our every want. Even worse, it has become a favorite form of entertainment. Yes, we entertain ourselves by spending money. Gone are the days when people spent their leisure time reading books, riding bikes, or entertaining friends for dinner. Now we feel obliged to spend money. We will fill our leisure hours wandering around shopping malls or surfing the internet, looking for a sale on something we don't need. Those with a real eye for bargains may substitute garage sales for shopping malls, but the root problem is the same. We have learned to fill our lives and our garages with stuff we don't really need.

The global economic meltdown in late 2008 was essentially the result of greed that caught up with us. Consumers and banking institutions found themselves holding mortgages and debts that were greater than the value of the assets they had financed. Compounding the crisis, jittery consumers reacted by cutting back on their spending, plunging our consumer-driven nation into recession.

Living Within Our Means

I have never been one to spend money I didn't have. My mother claims I still have the first dollar I ever earned. I had the blessing of learning from parents who modeled a frugal lifestyle. Consequently, I have never been in debt for a depreciable item or bought on credit anything I could not immediately pay off. I have always lived within my means, yet at times have come closer to the edge than I should have. One instance stands out.

I was twenty-one years old, engaged to Jerusha, and had decided I wanted to furnish our first apartment with something of quality. So, I went out and bought a brand new six-piece bedroom suite, a three-piece sectional couch, and an oak rocking chair for our living room. I also thought a memorable honeymoon was in order, so I purchased a week in Puerto Vallarta, Mexico, in a four-star hotel. When it was all said and done, though I had not incurred any debt, I had completely exhausted all my reserves.

One month before the wedding I attended a seminar at which the speaker addressed the topic of debt. I came away more determined than ever to avoid incurring debt. The problem was, I was about to get married and I was flat broke. When my father found out I was planning on driving the 2,500 miles from Toronto to San Diego with less than $100 in my pocket, he insisted on giving me some emergency funds. Though I didn't want the money, I reluctantly accepted it to ease his concerns, and tucked it into the corner of my wallet, determined not to spend money I didn't really have.

Were it not for a few generous gifts of cash tucked away in the wedding cards, I'm not sure I would have made it home debt-free. Fortunately, I learned through that experience that living with no financial margin is not living within my means.

The Freedom of Saying No

Over the years, Jerusha and I have learned to say no to many things we could have easily justified and afforded. A few years ago, right around the time we both turned fifty, we jokingly observed that in our bedroom we had nine different pieces of furniture, none of which matched. It's not that we couldn't afford to buy something new if we had wanted to. It's just that it had never been a high priority to us. It wasn't until we moved from Toronto to Kansas City the following year that we decided to finally replace our twenty-year collection of mismatched furniture with a new, matching set.

Saying no to consumerism has been liberating: We don't need to continually upgrade. We don't have to stop at a coffee shop every two hours when we're traveling. We don't need to see the latest movie as soon as it hits the theatres. Renting movies is just fine. And we don't need a giant screen TV to enjoy it at home, either.

Something Better Than Living Within Your Means

But there's something even better than living within our means. It's living below our means. It's not just saying no to certain things to stay out of debt and have something to put into savings. It's intentionally choosing to live with even less than what might seem to be legitimate so we can invest more in eternal kingdom pursuits.

I still have a long way to go when it comes to living like this. Though we drive a nine-year-old car, I find myself all too easily thinking about replacing it with a new one, even though mine looks and runs great. I live in a beautiful four-bedroom house with a triple garage and more square footage than we need. But now that the mortgage is paid off, checking the latest real estate listings in my neighborhood has become an all too common distraction. Since I can afford to buy something nicer and still live within my means, why not?

In the article "Choosing Contentment," author and CEO Phil Clemens described the impact of a decision he and his wife made years ago to live below their means.

> As Chief Executive Officer of the Clemens Family Foundation, a corporation with annual revenue that exceeds $1 billion and 4,000 members, people often

> have preconceived ideas of what my life is like, where I live and generally what I am like. When they get to know me, they often find their ideas were way off base.
>
> Shortly after I became CEO a very unusual thing happened which made me realize everything I do will be examined. One night, without my knowledge, an employee followed me home from work, just to see where I lived. The next day, he told some of his fellow-workers that they actually lived in nicer houses than the CEO!
>
> Several of our neighbors were minority employees who worked at the company and proudly told other employees that they lived on the same street as the CEO!

Rather than living in a house that fits the salary and stature of a CEO, the Clemenses have intentionally chosen a modest lifestyle, living in a house and driving a car that does not distinguish them from the average employee. Why? He explained:

> We generally give away between 50 and 70 percent of our income and try to live on about 20 percent, knowing the rest will go to paying our taxes.... We don't try to compare what we have or what we give to others since this is a very personal matter. We believe this is what God has called us to do and we

> will need to give an accounting of what we did with what He gave us.[18]

Here's a couple who have chosen to live well below their means, not as a demonstration of sacrifice or false humility, but simply because they want to have more to invest in things that will last much longer than houses and cars.

Called to Poverty?

Perhaps all this talk of spending less and giving more has you wondering whether the lifestyle I've described demands that followers of Christ take a vow of poverty. Not only has this not been our experience, I see nothing in Scripture that mandates it should be. There is nothing wrong with material possessions when they are used for the glory of God. What's more, because God loves to open the windows of heaven on those who use His resources rightly, it makes sense that some of the best givers have themselves become prosperous people.

If this is true, how do we determine the proper balance between wealth and generous giving? And how should believers who have less, view those who, for whatever reason, seem to have a whole lot more than they do? ■

Growing Outside the Box

"Be doers of the Word, and not hearers only" (James 1:22).

1. Choose one of the following words to describe your current debt load: crushing; unmanageable; manageable; light; non-existent.

2. If you would describe your current debt load as heavier than manageable, what tangible step will you take to begin extricating yourself from that weight?

3. Choose one of the following to describe your current lifestyle.

    - Living beyond my means
    - Living within my means
    - Living below my means

    Based on your answer, how is God is prompting you to move toward a simpler lifestyle?

4. Read Matthew 6:19–21 in preparation for the next chapter. What does it teach about giving, saving, and wise investing?

PART 3

GROWTH GIVING: AMAZING ADVENTURE OR IMPOSSIBLE DREAM?

The Incredible Returns on a Generous Life

12 IS GOD OPPOSED TO WEALTH?

The musical *Fiddler on the Roof* centers on Tevye, a Jewish peasant. In one of his many talks with God, Tevye ponders the question of wealth and poverty. One particularly long day as he is pulling his milk cart home from work, he bemoans that his horse is lame and that, for some unknown reason, God has ordained him to be poor. Tevye sings of how good life would be if only he were wealthy and asks God what harm there could possibly be in making him rich.

Old Tevye is not alone in his assumption that poverty is part of God's eternal plan for His people. Some believers feel the same way, as evidenced by their tendency to disguise the wealth they do have, envy wealth they don't have, and dream of wealth they'd like to have.

Enjoying What God Gives

Back in the 1990s when our family lived in France, Jerusha and I began to save for a dishwasher. We entertained a lot of people in our home, and after six years of washing dishes by hand, we decided it was time for some help. After months of saving and researching the best appliance for the money, we purchased a sturdy Whirlpool. We were excited. We had worked hard to save the money. We had found what we thought was a great machine for a great price. And we wanted to share our joy with someone. The problem was we worried how some of our Christian friends would respond. We knew that, for at least some, our purchase would be met with silent judgment. Perhaps we were too concerned about what others thought, but our perceptions were based on years of experience. How many times had we heard judgmental statements about someone else's vacation plans—"Must be nice to be able to afford a trip like that!"—or someone's purchase—"Do you know how much that thing must have cost?" How many times had we ourselves been guilty of such judgments?

In the end, I called up my best non-Christian buddy and told him. Somehow, I knew he would understand, be happy with me, and be thrilled to come over and help me fill my new dishwasher with some dirty dishes.

Our experience with the dishwasher purchase is a sad commentary on how far some of us as Christians have drifted from what God Himself says about healthy attitudes toward money and possessions. We believers cannot honestly enjoy the things God gives us richly to enjoy (1 Timothy 6:17) because of the notion that believers shouldn't have wealth, or if they do, at least they shouldn't enjoy it. Not only are such attitudes unbiblical, they risk spoiling God's plan for His children, not to be poor, but to be wealthy forever.

God Is Not Opposed to Wealth

Some of us need to correct our thinking about how God views wealth. In the first place, He is not against it. He does not treat it like something filthy that makes His nostrils flare in revulsion. God is, in fact the Creator and

Giver of wealth. To the ancient Israelites He said, "It is [God] who gives you the ability to produce wealth" (Deuteronomy 8:18). It is inconceivable then that God would be against something He willingly gave to His own people. To the apostle Paul's young protégé, Timothy, He gave instruction concerning the wealthier members in his congregation, making the rather surprising statement that God "richly provides us with everything for our enjoyment" (1 Timothy 6:17). Many Christians might be shocked to hear that when God chooses to bless someone with wealth, He wants them to enjoy it, not hide it or feel guilty about it. Not only that, but God wants them to enjoy it forever, not just in this life.

Here is some of Jesus's best-known advice about money and possessions:

> "Do not lay up for yourselves treasures on earth, where moth and rust destroy and where thieves break in and steal, but lay up for yourselves treasures in heaven, where neither moth nor rust destroys and where thieves do not break in and steal. For where your treasure is, there your heart will be also" (Matthew 6:19–21, ESV).

These verses contain at least two truths that we often miss, but which are of critical importance if we are ever to be convinced to obey what He is saying.

Accumulate Wealth...

The first truth from that passage is that Jesus wants us to accumulate treasure. The idea that God is against the accumulation of wealth is simply untrue. He is not against accumulating wealth; He is against losing it. The idea that God wants His followers to be poor could not be further from the truth. God is not telling us to give away earthly treasures because He wants to divest us of anything of value. God is deeply interested in what we give away while we're here on earth because He knows what a difference it will make in what we have in heaven.

...In the Right Place

Our problem when it comes to what God said about money is that we only hear half of it. We hear "Do not lay up for yourselves treasure on earth" and quit listening. We think God is a killjoy. We think He wants us to be penniless have-nots. Yet such an idea could not be further from the truth. It is nothing but a lie straight from hell.

Don't forget that Satan has always been the master of half-truths. He took God's prohibition to Adam and Eve against eating from one tree and suggested God didn't want them to eat from any tree. Then, referring to the consequences of eating, he affirmed that they would understand good and evil, but denied that they would die.

Satan does the same when it comes to you and me. I can just imagine his rant: *God doesn't want you to save up treasures on earth? You've gotta be kidding! He is so unreasonable. God wants to deprive you of enjoying life. You deserve more toys. You've worked hard for it.*

He plays the same game of half-truths with our youth when it comes to their sexual purity, convincing them that God is a pleasure-stealing ogre by asking them to abstain from sex before marriage. Yet God isn't against sexual pleasure. After all, He created it. He wants people to enjoy it to the maximum—which is exactly why God tells them to wait. To have sexual intimacy outside of marriage is to destroy the pure enjoyment of it. It is like pulling a half-baked cake from the oven and eating it under the misguided notion that if it's good when it's fully baked, it will be even better if eaten prematurely.

Enjoying Wealth Forever

In a similar way, the enemy has succeeded in convincing many people that God is against money and the accumulation of wealth. That is simply not true. The truth is He wants us to accumulate riches and He knows if we put them in the wrong place, we'll lose everything. Giving away earthly treasure is all about storing it up in a different location. When Jesus said, "Give it away," it was so that we can "Send it ahead." It's as if He said, "Don't put it all in an earthly investment where you'll lose it. Rather, move it to a heavenly investment where it will be preserved for you forever."

Years ago, at the advice of a financial planner, I put $10,000 into a fund he highly recommended. Since then, it has continually disappointed me. In the intervening years, it has not once been worth the value of the original investment. In fact, today it is barely worth the paper it is written on. While I've not always done so poorly, this transaction is a good reminder to me of what will ultimately happen to all wealth stored up on earth: it will be lost.

Unlike earthly investments, heavenly investments can never be lost. If I invest my earthly resources in endeavors of eternal value, they do not cease to be mine. Rather, they become mine to enjoy forever.

The Ultimate Insider Trading Tip

From time to time we hear of people who go to jail for profiting from what is referred to as insider trading. This white-collar crime involves obtaining confidential information about companies and stocks that are about to see a significant increase or decrease in value, and trading those stocks before the information becomes available to the public, thus making huge profits based on insider knowledge.

One of many such examples was the sentencing of a forty-year-old Toronto man who, along with his business partner, was accused of a major insider-trading scheme. The first man was sentenced to thirty-nine months in jail for his crime, while his alleged co-conspirator committed suicide shortly before he was to be arrested. Over a period of fourteen years, the pair netted almost $9 million in illegal profits based on knowledge they had surreptitiously gathered from documents at the law office where one of the men worked as a lawyer.[19]

Imagine how wealthy you could become if it were legally possible to know beforehand what stocks were going to skyrocket and then buy them. That's the idea in the advice Jesus offered us in this passage. Knowing the temporal wealth of this earth would one day become absolutely worthless, He urged us to divest ourselves of the wealth that will not stand the test of time and to reinvest it in eternal endeavors that will one day pay handsome returns.

As Christians, we have insider knowledge of a worldwide upheaval that will render the world's currency useless at Christ's return or when we die, whichever comes first. Everything that has not been converted to heaven's currency will be lost. Wisdom suggests we should not keep any more of the soon-to-be useless currency than we need to tide us over until then.

Will I Own Anything in Heaven?

The second oft-missed truth from Matthew 6:19–21 is this: Not only does Jesus want us to accumulate treasure, He wants us to accumulate it for ourselves. At first glance, this thought seems so selfish that we may have a difficult time believing He said it. Yet He did. He exhorted us to "lay up *for yourselves* treasure in heaven," and then, referring to that heavenly treasure, added "for where *your treasure* is, there your heart will be also" (emphasis mine). Jesus indicated this heavenly treasure would be ours to keep.

The apostle Paul made a similar affirmation to Timothy about wealthy believers. After saying that God "richly provides us with everything to enjoy," Paul told them how to enjoy it: "As for the rich… charge them… to do good, to be rich in good works, to be generous and ready to share, thus storing up treasure *for themselves* as a good foundation for the future…" (1 Timothy 6:17–19, ESV, emphasis mine). God clearly teaches that earthly resources successfully converted to heaven's currency will be ours to enjoy forever.

Not only can our financial assets be converted to eternal treasure, everything we do has the potential of eternal reward that will accrue to our benefit. In 1678, John Bunyan wrote Pilgrim's Progress in an English prison. He penned:

> Whatever good thing thou dost for Him, if done according to the Word, …is laid up for thee as treasure in chests and coffers, to be brought out to be rewarded before both men and angels, to *thy eternal comfort*[20] (emphasis mine).

If you have been a Christian long enough, you've probably heard someone say that all rewards we might receive in heaven will be cast back at the feet of Jesus in gratitude for all He has done for us. This claim seems to be based on a single verse in Revelation 4:10 that speaks of the twenty-four elders falling in worship before God and casting their crowns at His feet. From that isolated event some have jumped to the conclusion that all heavenly rewards we might receive will be turned back over to God. Personally, I don't see any evidence for it in that verse, much less in the many others that seem to teach otherwise. The most logical explanation for the elders placing their crowns at His feet is simply that it was an expression of submission or reverence to the King of the universe, much the same way we might remove our hats in the presence of someone important. If God expected us to turn over to Him all the rewards waiting for us in heaven, He would not have told us to lay them up in heaven for ourselves.

Do I Own Anything on Earth?

Not only did Jesus say that what we invest in heaven will be ours forever, He also said that what we have right now on earth is not ours at all. This angered some of

Jesus's listeners. We're told in Luke 16:14 that "The Pharisees, who loved money, heard all this and were sneering at Jesus." The Pharisees were the religious leaders of the day. They should have loved God. They should have loved people. And they should have loved the idea of putting away eternal wealth in heaven. But instead, they loved money—here and now. And because they loved their wallets, they detested the implications of what Jesus said on this subject. Don't underestimate the power of possessions to keep a person from hearing spiritual truth. The more important money is to a person, the more difficult it is for him to hear what God has to say about his resources.

Listen to what Jesus said that made them deride Him:

> "Whoever can be trusted with very little can also be trusted with much, and whoever is dishonest with very little will also be dishonest with much. So if you have not been trustworthy in handling worldly wealth, who will trust you with true riches? And if you have not been trustworthy with someone else's property, who will give you property of your own? No one can serve two masters. Either you will hate the one and love the other, or you will be devoted to the one and despise the other. You cannot serve both God and money" (Luke 16:10–13).

This was jaw-dropping truth, and they didn't like it.

Jesus contrasts "worldly wealth" with heaven's wealth—what He calls "true riches." The implication of that comparison is clear: the stuff we accumulate here isn't real. It's fool's gold. It sparkles like the real thing, but compared to what heaven offers, it's fake. No wonder the Pharisees snorted. Jesus called what they loved phony.

On a trip to a war-torn central Asian country, a friend of mine came across some rare American coins at an open market, one of which was a silver dollar from 1796. He paid the vendor five dollars for it, brought it home, and gave it to me as a gift. Since he and I were both skeptical that rare American coins could be found in such places and sold for such prices, we figured it was a forgery. But, just for the fun of it, I loaned it to a collector friend of mine to evaluate without telling him the backstory. He excitedly told me it could be worth upwards of $500. Later, after examining it closely, he called me back and, with disappointment in his voice, told me the coin wasn't genuine. Though by all appearances it looked like the real thing, he discovered one misplaced letter on the edge of the coin which gave it away. Only an expert could tell it was fake.

Jesus was that expert when it came to earthly currencies, and He told His listeners this troubling truth: It's not real. Then He made another shocking statement. It's not yours!

He called it someone else's property: "If you have not been trustworthy *with someone else's property…*" (emphasis mine). No wonder the Pharisees were upset. First, He told them their money was counterfeit. Then He told them it wasn't actually their money. This is not what most people, ourselves included, want to hear. We like to think it's ours. We like to think, and we tend to live as if, our houses and our cars and our investments are ours. But they're not. The Master has simply left these things in our care for us to manage to see whether He can trust us with true riches.

Let this truth sink in: You are not the owner of what is currently in your possession. You are merely the manager. And like the money manager in Luke 16 who was called in to give an account of how he had been spending the owner's money, we too will one day do the same. Grasping that truth alone will change how you spend and what you give. Furthermore, when you remember it is not yours in the first place, it's easier to give it away.

The Pharisees, who loved money, were shocked by this assertion. But equally shocking is what Jesus then said about the "true riches" of heaven. He called it "property of your own." A paraphrase of these two verses might read like this: "If you have not been trustworthy in handling earthly wealth which isn't real and doesn't belong to you, who will give you the true riches of heaven as property of your own?"

Did you hear what Jesus said? We have it all backwards! We think what we have on earth is the real thing, and that it's ours to do with as we please. And we think whatever wealth might await us in heaven will be given back to Jesus out of worship and thanksgiving. But it's just the opposite. Earth's wealth isn't real and it isn't ours, while heaven's wealth is more real than anything we have ever known and it will be ours for the keeping—property of our very own.

If Jesus's words were misunderstood and offensive to the religious people of His day, we should not be surprised that the same is true today. The likelihood of offense is high in a world like ours where great wealth has become increasingly commonplace, reaching levels unimagined by previous generations. Furthermore, great wealth is no longer the exclusive domain of a privileged few in the unbelieving world. Many Christians have gotten in on the game as well. Visit the Sunday morning parking lot of the average church in America to see that we're doing okay when it comes to wealth, at least as measured by the cars we drive. What would Jesus say about that? Does He want us to get rid of all our high-end cars?

Does God Want Me to Sell My BMW?

Back when I was a child, "good" Christians didn't drive Lincolns or Cadillacs or Mercedes or any other high-end car for that matter. To have wealth, or at least to display it, was almost a sure sign of a Christian whose priorities were out of whack. I'm not sure how we explained the existence of wealthy saints of old like Abraham and Job. I just knew great wealth was something a Christian shouldn't have, and if he had it, he better hide it.

So, what is God's view of believers' wealth? Is it wrong to be a wealthy follower of Jesus? Is it okay to drive a Lincoln or a Lexus? Or should we limit ourselves to a good used Chevy or Ford? What is the maximum amount believers should have tied up in a house? How many vacations a year is acceptable and to what destinations? What class of hotel should we stay in? How often should we eat out, and at what kind of restaurants?

Some of us as Christians have a hard time living with ambiguity. This is especially true in western society where we tend to see things in black and white. A person is either right or wrong, Republican or Democrat, for or against. So, when it comes to the issue of Christians and their possessions, the tendency is to set some clear boundaries defining what is acceptable and what is not.

The problem with such an approach to money and possessions is its subjectivity. We arbitrarily determine how much is too much (usually based on how much we have) and silently sit in judgment on those who cross the line we established. It is interesting that Jesus not only used the illustration of weights and measures to indicate God's repayment plan for generosity, but He also used the same illustration to describe His repayment plan for those who judge others. "Do not judge, or you too will be judged," He warned. "For in the same way you judge others, you will be judged, and with the measure you use, it will be measured to you" (Matthew 7:1–2).

God most certainly will not use my standard of judgment when it comes to how He assesses the wealth of my Christian brothers and sisters. He might, however, use my own standard on me, so I'd better be careful how I judge. I have grown increasingly tired of the critical attitudes I encounter in the Christian world when it comes to how we view the wealth of fellow believers. I am of the conviction that it is truly none of my business to rule on the spirituality of other people based on the limited external indicators I have to work with, such as the kind of car they drive or the size of house they live in. Since I do not have all the facts, I cannot and should not make the call.

What Would Jesus Drive?

But God will make the call, and the question still remains as to what He thinks about the car I drive, the house I live in, the vacations I take, the investments I make, and every detail of how I choose to manage His resources.

Determining how much of His wealth should be used for personal benefit versus how much should be invested in eternal endeavors is something each of us must decide, considering His desire for us to be truly rich forever. God does not operate by rigid rules. God does not judge based on a policy manual outlining what kinds of cars believers can drive or how much square footage makes for an acceptable earthly dwelling. What is appropriate for one person is not necessarily appropriate for another. But make no mistake about it, God is highly interested in how each of His children manages what He has entrusted to them, and He will determine whether we have managed His resources appropriately.

Spoiling God's Eternal Plan

So, what is the answer to Tevye's question about God's plans and earthly wealth? God's grand plan spanning eternity is that each of us be wealthy men and women—wealthy with riches that will make earthly treasures look like household garbage by comparison. And the only thing that will spoil this divine plan is our failure to convert this world's wealth into heaven's currency.

One of the most gripping accounts of someone who used worldly wealth for the benefit of others was captured in the book (and movie by the same title) Schindler's List. It tells the story of a wealthy German industrialist, Oscar Schindler, who used his businesses and wealth to save more than a thousand Polish Jews from Nazi extermination camps. He accomplished this by hiring them in his factories and literally purchasing their lives from the military and political officials who had planned to exterminate them.

As the war drew to a close, Schindler, himself a Nazi Party member and a self-described "profiteer of slave labor," was forced to flee the advancing Red Army. Although the SS guards were ordered to "liquidate" the Jews of Brinnlitz, Czechoslovakia, Schindler persuaded them to return to their families as men and not as murderers. In the aftermath, he packed a car in the night and bid farewell to his Jewish workers. They gave him a letter explaining that he was not a criminal to them, together with a ring secretly made from a worker's gold dental bridge and engraved with a Talmudic quotation: "Whoever saves one life saves the world entire."[21] Schindler was touched but deeply ashamed, feeling he could have done more to save many more lives. Pondering how many more he could have saved, he wept over what might have been had he liquidated more of his possessions or not been so wasteful.

I wonder how many tears will be shed when we one day stand on the brink of eternity and realize how much more of our earthly wealth we could have invested in eternal souls but didn't. May we not ignore that the grand eternal plan of God is to make us and others unfathomably and eternally rich through the proper investment of the earthly resources He has given us to manage. ■

Growing Outside the Box

"Be doers of the Word, and not hearers only" (James 1:22).

1. What did you find surprising, new, or perhaps unsettling about how God views wealth? Why?
2. Why does there seem to be so much misunderstanding on the part of believers about how God views money and possessions?
3. What are some general biblical principles that can guide your decisions about what is an appropriate or inappropriate use of money for earthly purposes? (In other words, how do we decide rightly how much we should spend on a car, house, or vacation in light of eternity?)
4. How will you allow the truths in this chapter to affect how you use the resources with which you've been entrusted? What, if anything, needs to change?

13 DON'T EAT THAT MARSHMALLOW...YET

In the late 1960s, researchers at Stanford University conducted an experiment in delayed gratification to measure the correlation between a child's level of self-control and his or her ultimate ability to succeed in life.

The children were led into a room, empty of distractions, where a treat of their choice (a marshmallow or cookie) was placed on a table. The children were instructed that they could eat the marshmallow, but if they waited for fifteen minutes until the monitor returned, they would be rewarded with a second marshmallow. Some children would cover their eyes with their hands or would turn their chairs so they couldn't see the treat. Others would begin kicking the desk or stroking the marshmallow. Some, the minority, simply ate the marshmallow as soon as the monitor left. Another group held out for a while, but not long enough to receive the second one when the researcher returned. Of the 600 children ages four through six, one-third deferred gratification long enough to get the second marshmallow.

The study then followed up on these same children in their adult years to see how they had fared in terms of life outcomes, as measured by SAT scores, educational attainment, body mass index, and various other life measures. Those children who had been able to resist eating the lone marshmallow in favor of the added benefit of a second one later were also generally more successful as adults in terms of relationships, education, and careers. The researchers concluded that there is a correlation between the ability to delay gratification and the ability to do well in life.

While more recent studies[22] questioned the conclusions of the original study on grounds that it failed to take into account the relative impact of poverty and affluence, the fact remains that the ability to delay gratification does affect one's success in life.

What's in It for Me?

There is a powerful motivator in my quest to become increasingly generous toward eternal pursuits. It is a conviction that, by delaying my desire to gratify myself with material things in this life, I can make more long-term investments that will one day yield a much greater return. I am not ashamed to tell you that I am looking forward to my eternal wealth in heaven.

Some who read these words may have difficulty with that thought. Isn't it selfish and greedy to desire wealth, even if it is the true and pure wealth of heaven? Shouldn't I serve and obey God with no thought for what I have to gain from it? Isn't it more than enough that I'll be with Jesus for eternity, without wanting heaven's riches as well? As noble as those sentiments may appear, I believe they reflect an inaccurate understanding of the teachings of Scripture.

A Heaven of Clouds and Harps

At least part of our problem with the idea of rewards may be a deficient understanding of the real and tangible nature of heaven.

It is admittedly difficult for us to conceive of a place we've never been, especially when it is so unlike our existence that words fail to describe it. Furthermore, the idea of a material heaven that in any way resembles life as we know it seems almost carnal, unspiritual, and unworthy of consideration. Somehow people have developed a view of heaven that consists of little more than clouds, harps, and worship services. Because the angels cry "holy, holy, holy" night and day, we envision heaven will be something like an eternal worship service where we stand and sing for hours on end while looking at the backs of the heads of the people in front of us.

Such a view of heaven not only strikes me as incredibly monotonous, but it does a great injustice both to the real nature of worship and to what Scripture reveals to us about heaven. Before you accuse me of heresy, please understand I did not say, nor do I believe, worshipping Jesus for eternity will be incredibly monotonous. What I did label monotonous is the view of worship that limits it to standing in rows and singing songs for eternity—a view which unfortunately has been conditioned by what happens across America at about 11 a.m. on Sunday mornings and has been labeled "the worship service."

God has created a material universe that calls us to not just an hour of worship but a life of continual worship that goes far beyond standing in rows and singing songs. As I write these words, I am seated at a table looking out the window of a beautiful summer home nestled by a crystal-clear lake. I believe God made this little corner of creation to inspire in me worship of the true and living God. I am not here to worship the creation. I am here to worship the Creator of this magnificent creation. The lake home I am sitting in is a masterpiece built by some of the finest craftsmen in the building industry. I believe God made people with the ability to design and produce beautiful architecture to inspire in us the worship of a God who is the Designer by His very nature. Where people have gone wrong is in worshipping the creature and the works of their hands, rather than the magnificent Creator whose works were intended to point us to Him.

Heaven May Surprise You

I say all this to explain my conviction that heaven will be surprisingly more material than many of us have probably imagined, and all of it will be designed to ignite our hearts in joyful worship. The physical world we live in now is merely a foretaste of the glorious eternal state to which we are headed. Heaven will be a perfect, unending, sin-free, and tangible place not unlike the world as God originally conceived it. Indeed, the first abode of humans before the arrival of sin was a physical world where God and the people He made walked together in perfect harmony. Why then can we not imagine such a world again?

The descriptions we have of the eternal state are material indeed, complete with trees, rivers, fruit, precious stones, streets, buildings, and governments. In some respects, it is surprisingly reminiscent of Eden. God seems to purposely make a link between the two by including the Tree of Life in His description of the heavenly city in Revelation 21–22. That mysterious life-giving tree, present in the Garden of Eden at the beginning of time, is never again mentioned until the final book of the Bible. It is almost as if God, in creating our eternal dwelling place, is restoring man to the paradise that was lost in Eden.

A Real Place with Real Rewards

Heaven is not only described in tangible terms, but also in rewarding terms. Though some may consider the idea of rewards to be unspiritual, we need to realize the idea came from God. Noted author Bruce Wilkinson, in *The Life God*

Rewards, detailed the many places in Scripture where God rewards His children for a wide variety of things: concern for the poor and needy (Luke 14:13–14); seeking Him through fasting (Matthew 6:17–18) and prayer (Matthew 6:6); whole-hearted service (Colossian 3:22–24); suffering for His sake (Luke 6:22–23); and yes, using one's material resources for kingdom purposes (1Timothy 6:17).[23]

Pastor and author Erwin Lutzer said that while rewards will be part of our experience in heaven, not everyone will receive them. "Salvation is guaranteed to those who accept Christ by faith; rewards are not. Entering heaven is one thing; having a possession there is quite another. One is the result of faith; the other, the reward for faith plus obedience."[24]

Jesus was so committed to the concept of rewarding righteous behavior that He said even the seemingly inconsequential act of offering a glass of water to someone in His name would not go without a reward (Matthew 10:42). Personally, I'm not much of a water drinker. I prefer something with a little more taste. Water is so plain and so cheap that, in our part of the world at least, it's virtually free. What Jesus was essentially saying was this: "Name the most simple, basic gesture you can think of. If you do even that out of love for Me, you can count on a reward waiting for you."

Do We Do It for The Reward?

Do we do these things for the reward, or do we do them for the One we love? My answer to the question is yes! I love Jesus so much that I would serve Him simply because He is magnificent in every way, and the only Being in the universe worthy of my worship. But that does not eliminate my motivation to obtain the rewards He offers me. Not only can I hardly wait to see Jesus, I am also eager to see what He has prepared for me. He himself incited that kind of anticipation when He said, "No eye has seen, no ear has heard, and no mind has imagined what God has prepared for those who love him" (1 Corinthians 2:9, NLT). Will those rewards detract from my adoration of Him? Not at all. Instead, they will only serve to further elicit from me the love and wonder that already fill my heart when I consider His gracious, loving character.

God is not threatened by the possibility that His gifts to me will steal my heart from worshipping Him, any more than I am threatened by the gifts I offer Jerusha from time to time. Not once in all our years of marriage have my gifts to her diminished her love for me. Nor have they been the reason for her love. She does not love me for the gifts, yet the gifts do enhance her expressions of love for me. It is almost as if they are an added opportunity for her to express her delight in the gift-giver.

Similarly, if God offers us gifts, whether to reward us or simply to express His love for us, it is not because He is trying to buy our love. Rather it is simply an expression of His gracious nature, and an added opportunity for us, His bride, to in turn express our delight in Him.

Where Your Treasure Is...

Our human nature causes us to be attracted to things we consider valuable. For several years while growing up, my younger son, Nathan, had a keen interest in Ford Mustangs. For some reason, he considered them valuable—so much so that it was as if they had taken over the highways. Because of how much he valued Mustangs, he tended to notice every single one of them on the road. It was as if he had a built-in Mustang radar that allowed his eyes to detect any Mustang within a hundred feet of him.

God knows that the best way to get our radar locked in on heaven is to get our valuables up there ahead of us. How do we do that? We take our most valuable commodities—time and money—and we invest significant amounts of them in heaven. This is precisely what Jesus had in mind when He said, "…store up for yourselves treasures in heaven… For where your treasure is, there your heart will be also" (Matthew 6:20–21).

Why didn't Jesus just tell us to work harder at loving Him? Why didn't He say, "For where your Savior is, there your heart will be also"? Shouldn't that be our driving motivation? Shouldn't He be our only motivation? Well, perhaps in a perfect world, the answer would be yes. But we don't live in a perfect world and Jesus knows that if our money is not turned heavenward, our hearts will not be either.

Every month, the first checks I write are the ones that go to the support of our local church and of the cross-cultural workers all over the world whom we, as a couple, have chosen to partner with. We have made substantial investments not only here in the United States and Canada, but in more than a dozen countries around the world. We have had a part in blessing God's workers, spreading the gospel, and making disciples in many places. These are by far the most profitable investments we have made during our earthly existence, and they are what keep our hearts' radar locked on heaven.

Equal to those investments are the ones we have made in the people around us. I really mean that. Supporting a widow who is struggling to raise her family while holding down two jobs is not a burden to us. It's an investment. And a joyful one at that. Providing gas money for a neighbor who has just incurred significant travel expenses to attend to a tragic loss in his family is not wasted money. It is an expression of a generous God—and it will not go unrewarded.

The only way I can keep my heart from being seduced by earthly possessions is to convert a significant amount of what God has entrusted to me into heaven's currency. To encourage me to do that more and more, God tells me that such faith-inspired behavior will be rewarded.

An Unparalleled Return on Investment

One day Jesus was talking to His disciples about the powerful pull of possessions and how they can keep a person from heaven. In response to this teaching, Peter piped up with a rather amazing statement: "We have left everything to follow you! What then will there be for us?" (Matthew 19:27). On the surface at least, his question appeared self-serving. He was essentially asking Jesus what would be the pay-back for the sacrifices they were making to follow Him. One might expect such a question to elicit a stinging rebuke from Jesus in the order of "Get behind me, Satan!" (Matthew 16:23) or something similar. Instead, Jesus answered Peter's question with an equally astounding promise:

> "Truly I tell you, at the renewal of all things, when the Son of Man sits on his glorious throne, you who have followed me will also sit on twelve thrones, judging the twelve tribes of Israel. And everyone who has left houses or brothers or sisters or father or mother or wife or children or fields for my sake will receive a hundred times as much and will inherit eternal life" (Matthew 19:28–29).

The reward for giving up all to follow Jesus was a prominent place in the Messiah's government for each of the apostles. But did you catch the rest? For everyone who has made personal and material sacrifices for the sake of the Lord Jesus, He promised a one hundred-fold return on their investment. Do the math. That's a 10,000 percent return! I don't know whether Jesus was speaking in hyperbole to make a point or whether He was giving the actual rate of return on investment. Either way, it's out of this world, and I'm eager to see what it will be.

From Cottage to Gold-Plated Mansion

I remember as a child singing the hymn, "Mansion Over the Hilltop." It spoke of the glorious gold and silver-lined dwelling places that await believers in heaven. I'm not sure where the songwriter got his idea of gold-plated, silver-lined mansions, but I must admit the idea never particularly struck a chord with me.

As the years went by, I began to hear some preachers who poked holes in the heavenly mansion idea, claiming the word Jesus used in John 14 really means *apartments*. Perhaps these same preachers didn't like the idea of rewards either. But whatever their motivation, I can assure you the idea of heavenly apartments appealed to me even less than silver mansions. I have lived in numerous apartments and none of them were particularly heavenly. The idea of living in a heavenly high-rise, packed in with millions of other Christians above, below, and beside me honestly doesn't sound like heaven.

The Greek word Jesus used, *moné*, does not define what our heavenly home will look like. It's best translated *abode* or *dwelling* and simply refers to a place where someone lives. Here on earth that can be just about anything. From the cardboard shacks in an impoverished slum to the breathtaking mansions of the rich and famous, dwelling can be used to describe them all. What often determines the nature of the dwelling is the neighborhood in which it is found. In the greater Toronto region, where I spent over a decade of my life, the names "Rosedale" and "Rexdale" conjure up two completely different pictures of dwelling places. One is at the top end of the housing scale; the other is not.

In a similar way, it is the neighborhood that will define the nature of our dwellings in heaven. Heaven's homes will be spectacular because heaven is spectacular. I don't know whether they will be gold, silver, or some heavenly substance we've never heard of, but I am sure of this: they will be more amazing than anything we have ever laid eyes on. They will be real. They will be lived in. They will be part and parcel of our reward. And, the treasures we choose to send on ahead of us may very well become part of the budget and building materials Christ will use in His preparation of our heavenly place.

To be honest with you, I can hardly wait. Like the child who says no to a marshmallow now in hope of a greater reward later, I too strain to curb my appetite for the world's fleeting treasures out of a conviction that the God who promises rewards to His children will be true to His Word. And, when someday I open my eyes to behold the wonders of all He has prepared for me, I am sure heaven's delights will only serve to inspire me to love and worship Him even more.

Deferring Gratification Just a Bit Longer

Most of those who have read this far have probably learned, like those youngsters with the marshmallows, to defer gratification in many ways because we hope for greater rewards. But for some of us, our timeline for cashing in on the rewards we've been anticipating is about twenty years too short. What I mean is this. Most of us will work and scrimp and save during the best years of our lives (probably the forty years between ages twenty and sixty) so we can enjoy the fruits of our labors and self-denial for our final twenty years. We live life as if retirement is the big reward. But it isn't. The truly big reward, the one that will make all of earth's finest wealth look like dime-store jewelry by comparison, is the one that's waiting for us just beyond this life.

Don't trade in your stale marshmallow a few years too early and settle for a mere two or three more. Keep your gaze averted from the marshmallow just a bit longer. Keep striving to convert as much of earth's wealth into heaven's currency. The return on investment will truly be astronomical. ■

Growing Outside the Box

"Be doers of the Word, and not hearers only" (James 1:22).

1. How has Christian terminology like "the worship service" and "the worship team" influenced your concept of what worship in heaven will be like?
2. How do you envision heaven?
3. How do you feel about the idea of receiving rewards in heaven? Does it make you excited or uncomfortable? Why?
4. What ideas do you have to "give a cup of cold water in Jesus name" to someone in your world this week?
5. What is something you can do today by faith, to defer gratification in this life, in anticipation of a far greater reward?

14 THE ULTIMATE PURPOSE OF GIVING

Jesus clearly indicated that the ultimate purpose of wealth and of life itself was not merely to enjoy the seventy or eighty years we might have on this earth. To live life and to use wealth in that way is to lose it forever.

But it is also short-sighted and dangerous to think that the ultimate purpose of wealth and of life on earth is merely to enrich myself for eternity. If I am simply deferring the enjoyment of life's pleasures now to have a posher dwelling place in heaven, all I'm doing is figuring out a way to live self-centeredly forever.

We were not created for ourselves, but for God. The apostle Paul said to the Colossian believers, "All things have been created through him and for him" (Colossians

1:16b, NASB). To the Romans, he wrote: "For from him and through him and to him are all things. To him be glory forever" (Romans 11:36, ESV). Life is not about my glory, but His.

The ultimate purpose of life, including a generous lifestyle, has to do with what Scripture refers to as "God's glory." Paul said, "…whether you eat or drink or whatever you do, do it all for the glory of God" (1 Corinthians 10:31). If eating and drinking are to serve that purpose, then certainly our giving should also. But what exactly does it mean to eat, to drink, or to give of our resources for the glory of God?

Created to Enjoy Him

The Westminster Catechism was written in 1647 to instruct believers in the essentials of the Christian faith. The first question asks: "What is the chief end of man?" To paraphrase, we might ask: "What were human beings created for?" The catechism gives a two-fold answer: "Man's chief end is to glorify God and to enjoy him forever."[25]

To glorify something and to enjoy it go hand in hand. To glorify means to extol the supreme value or virtue of something I enjoy. If I thought Switzerland was the most wonderful place on earth, and I spoke to you frequently of its incredible mountains, its picture-perfect villages, its exquisite cuisine, its crystal-clear lakes, its well-maintained infrastructure, its stable currency, and its hospitable people, you could say I glorified life in Switzerland.

To glorify God is to do just that. It is to extol the virtues and magnificence of the One who created us and the universe around us. It is to make Him look attractive by the way I speak about Him, the way I do my work, the way I love my spouse, the way I raise my children, the way I treat my neighbors—even by the way I spend my money. The best (and easiest) way to glorify God, is to do as the catechism says—"enjoy him" myself. When I enjoy God, I don't have to try hard to make Him look good. People are drawn to Him by virtue of how much I enjoy Him.

The ultimate purpose of life is to so enjoy the God of life that everything we do and say is an invitation to others to enjoy Him with us. To enjoy the glorious God who has created us is the essence of worship and the impetus for sharing Him with others. This is why we were created. God did not create us because He was lonely. Nor did He create us because He lacked anything. He created us for no other reason than He wanted to bring us and others into the eternal enjoyment of His glorious character.

This may seem rather self-centered on God's part unless we understand how truly enjoyable He is. He does not invite us to enjoy Him for His sake, but for our sakes. He does not desire our worship for His own benefit, but for ours. He loves to share Himself with us because He is so magnificent and delightful.

Sharing What We Enjoy Most

A few years ago, I was invited to take a night cruise with about a dozen other people on one of the many beautiful lakes in Canada's cottage country. As our boat slid across the smooth surface of the lake guided only by the lights of the shoreline, our collective attention was suddenly seized by a spectacular sight. Directly ahead of us there rose above the horizon the most massive orange lunar globe I have ever seen. Everyone in the boat let out a gasp of wonder and began saying to each other, "Look at that! Look at that! Isn't it incredible? I've never seen anything like it. Just look at it!"

What were we doing? Why were we telling each other to look at something we could all obviously see? The answer is simple. We were enjoying something spectacular and were inviting others into the enjoyment of it with us. I would have been greatly disappointed to have experienced such a magnificent sight if I had not had anyone to share it with. It is not out of selfishness that we invite others to share in that which is spectacular, glorious, and awe-inspiring. Rather, it is to enhance the full enjoyment of it.

So it is with God and His glory. Everything in creation was intended to point us to God as the glorious One behind it all. Though sin has seriously marred the beauty of His plan, it is still His intention to redeem His ruined creatures and draw them into the wonders of worshiping Him. Every delightful experience of life should point us to Him, provoking in us a "Look at that!" response. When we enjoy the delights of human love, the succulence of a well-prepared meal, the beauty of a sunset, or the peace of a loon calling across the expanse of a pristine lake, our hearts should be lifted in wonder and longing for the God who made it all. If life is that good, how incredible must be the God of life! We were created to enjoy Him now and forever, and the earth is filled with His glory in order to whet our appetites for eternity.

Created for Something More

But there is a significant problem with this picture. God is not worshiped by most of the world's people. Today, more than 2,000 years after Christ came and sacrificed His life to redeem his creation, roughly 90 percent of the world's people do not acknowledge Jesus Christ as God's only provision for sin. In many of the least-reached parts of the world, the percentage of those without Christ rises to more than 99 percent.[26]

If God created people to enjoy Him for all eternity, and yet over 6 billion people alive today are not enjoying Him and are destined to enter eternity forever separated from Him, then something must change.

This realization moved Jerusha and me many years ago to pursue a career in cross-cultural missions. We could not bear the thought that while we lived in a country where the gospel was freely available, there were places all over the world with virtually no knowledge of Jesus.

We understood we were created for more than to simply worship and enjoy God forever. We were created to invite others to enjoy Him with us. As author and pastor John Piper succinctly stated, "Missions exists because worship doesn't."[27]

Money and Missions

If the ultimate purpose of life is to enjoy God and to bring others into the enjoyment of Him, then it stands to reason that the goal of everything we do needs to feed into that purpose. The goal of giving, therefore, is to express our joy in God and to make it possible for others to also discover eternal joy in Him. Generous giving may accomplish many things, but at its core, it is a statement about the supreme value of knowing and enjoying God. Yes, giving is an expression of trust. It is a matter of obedience. Yes, it helps pay the utilities for the church building and the salary of those who have given themselves to vocational pastoral work. But the bottom line is that the giving of our resources is all about enjoying and proclaiming God's glory throughout the earth. How I spend the resources He has entrusted to me says something to those around me about what I believe is truly important.

Piper, whose books and messages have inspired millions to live sacrificially, asked this penetrating question:

> When was the last time someone asked you about the reason for the hope that is in you? That's what Peter said we should always be ready to give an answer for. Why don't people ask us about our hope?

The answer is probably that we look as if we hope in the same things they do.[28]

A Significant Hindrance to the Spread of the Gospel

I have been a vocational minister of the gospel for over 30 years. For roughly two-thirds of that time, as the president of Crossworld in Canada and more recently in the United States, I've helped to mobilize resources for reaching the world—both people and money.

Whenever I ask people about the greatest obstacle for them in considering cross-cultural ministry, by far the most common answer is money. Thousands of potential workers are deterred every year for lack of financial resources, or for fear of having to embark on the journey of financial support development. It seems they have heard enough horror stories and have read enough missionary prayer letter pleas for funds that many have decided to do something else with their lives. While some might argue that's all for the best because these people obviously lack the faith to be missionaries, I am not so quick to rush to this conclusion.

There is no doubt in my mind that the gospel enterprise is stunted in its growth because of insufficient financial resources. There are certainly other reasons, but this one is of primary importance. Studies indicate that only two to four cents of every charitable dollar given to the church in North America is spent to spread the gospel worldwide. I realize many who will read these pages do much better than that, but across the board this is the reality. World Vision president Richard Stearns wrote:

> The bottom line is that the commitment that American Christians, the wealthiest Christians in all history, are making to the world is just about 2% (of every charitable dollar)… In simpler terms, that amounts to about 6 pennies per person per day that we give through our churches to the rest of the world—*6 cents!*[29]

According to research commissioned by Ladder and conducted by OnePoll, "the average adult in the USA spends $1,497 a month on non-essential items... that's roughly $18,000 a year on things we can all do without."[30]

Another study of American spending habits revealed that Americans spend about 15 percent of their household income on things that they do not need in order to keep themselves amused.[31] The movie industry represents one example of such discretionary spending. The Bureau of Labor Statistics' 2016 Consumer Expenditure Survey revealed that North Americans spent $11.9 billion that year at the box office.[32] Add to that the $25.2 billion spent on renting and buying movies for home viewing, and the discretionary spending triples.[33]

By comparison, the contribution of American Christians to reaching the world outside their borders is about $2.5 billion per year.[34]

If the worldwide worship of our glorious God is the ultimate purpose of life, these statistics alone should tell us there is a problem. It helps explain why there are entire countries in the world today with almost no followers of Jesus and why more than 2.5 billion people today have never once heard the gospel.[35]

Getting the Right Perspective on Giving

The kind of generous giving that will resource and sustain the spread of the gospel to the billions who have still never heard, and the 6 billion who have yet to believe, will not be borne from guilt but only from grace. It will only come through people who enjoy God so much that all of life becomes aligned with the grand purpose of enjoying

Him and helping others to enjoy Him too. Spending their lives and resources in that great pursuit becomes the only logical thing to do. And it's not a burden. It's a pleasure.

What could have possibly motivated the dirt-poor believers of Macedonia to beg for the privilege of giving their last dollar to an offering even the apostle Paul didn't expect them to participate in? Paul answered like this: "the grace of our Lord Jesus Christ, that though he was rich, yet for your sake he became poor, so that you through his poverty might become rich" (2 Corinthians 8:9). It was the example of Christ Himself, the eternally rich Son of God who became the temporarily poor Son of man, in order to make others eternally rich.

It was the overwhelming joy that had been borne in the heart of Zacchaeus, a former greedy, crooked tax collector, that spurred him on to give away half of all he owned to the poor.

It was only a deeply grateful heart that could have caused a poor woman with only two small coins to her name to put them both in the temple treasury (Mark 12:42).

It was a heart overflowing with gratitude for the grace and forgiveness of her Lord Jesus that caused a sinful woman to enter the house of a Pharisee—one who disdained her—in order to pour costly perfume on Jesus's feet. Jesus Himself said: "…her sins, which are many, have been forgiven, for she loved much" (Luke 7:47, NASB).

The more we love and enjoy Him, the more natural it becomes for us to become exceptionally generous with our lives.

Where Should I Give My Money?

When I teach on giving, I'm sometimes asked how much of a household's giving should go to the local church. It is our personal practice and conviction, as husband and wife, that at least the first 10 percent of our income should go to our local church fellowship. Though I have no verse or chapter to prove it, I believe that since Christ loves the church and has entrusted to her the Great Commission to reach the world, the local church must have top priority in our giving. Any church that has a clear understanding of the ultimate purpose of life will in turn designate a significant percentage of their offerings for the spread of the gospel worldwide. That's the kind of church I want to be part of and give to.

More than thirty years ago, our sending church in California, under the leadership of Pastor David Jeremiah, decided to allocate 20 percent of the church's offerings to global missions. God has greatly blessed that commitment. Since that decision was made sometime in the early 1980s, the church's annual giving to world missions has grown from $200,000 to more than $3 million. God loves to bless churches committed to blessing the nations. And I love to give to a church like that—and 10 percent is only the starting point.

Blessing Those Outside the Local Church

I am also persuaded that believers should learn to give to causes above and beyond the needs of their local church. If 10 percent is merely the starting point of stewardship and not the ultimate expression of it, growth in giving allows us to become exceptionally generous to others. Followers of Jesus should be known as the most generous people in the world. Yet, I've heard more than a few people in the restaurant business say that a waiter's least favorite shift is the Sunday lunch shift, when gospel tracts are plentiful, but the tips are not. This should not be true of grace-filled believers.

As you might imagine, the financial support of cross-cultural gospel ministers is high on our list of priorities after giving to our local church. We look for those whom we have known to be faithful and effective where God has placed them, and we invest in the work God has called them to, whether domestic or international. This gives us a more personal sense of involvement in the Great Commission, and it also helps speed workers on their way. Today, while about a third of a missionary's support comes from the budgets of the local church, as much as 70 percent will come through family and friends. That's why we give, not only to our local church but to the missionaries and their sending agencies as well.

But our generosity must not be limited to causes that provide us with a charitable giving receipt. The day may not be far off when the incentive of a tax deduction for our generosity will disappear entirely. I want my giving to be without consideration for whether or not the government choses to encourage it. This perspective frees me to be more generous to neighbors, friends, or family members when needs arise.

When Jerusha sees a sale on fresh-picked cherries, she may buy extra to share with a neighbor. When someone new moves into our neighborhood, a gift of fresh flowers is a simple yet generous gesture. When a friend or family member can't afford a plane ticket to attend an important event, we have the capacity to help. The great advantage of growing to the point of giving away well beyond 10 percent is the freedom it gives to not only generously support the local church, but to freely bless others. More than that, when we understand what our purpose in life is, it just makes sense.

The worldwide proclamation of God's glory will be fully realized when God's people release His resources in glad worship of Him. Biblical money management and global mission go hand in hand. ■

Growing Outside the Box

"Be doers of the Word, and not hearers only" (James 1:22).

1. How much would you say you enjoy God? How have you enjoyed Him in the past week?
2. What are some tangible ways you could increase your enjoyment of God? If you're having trouble answering this question, think of how you grow in your enjoyment of something in other areas of life.
3. If the watching world were to assess what is truly important to you by observing how you spend your time and your money, what would they conclude?
4. Consider how you're currently investing your resources to get the gospel to the people and places that have little to no access. Is there any part of your discretionary spending (coffee shops, theatres, restaurants, media services, memberships, etc.) where God is nudging you to redirect those funds toward getting the gospel to those who have never heard it?

15 RICH MAN, POOR MAN

There is no greater opportunity to be rich forever than to invest your life—your time, talent, treasure—*everything*—in maximizing the visibility and enjoyment of God's magnificence. And there is no greater threat to laying hold of those riches than the desire to spend your life on yourself. That threat is so great that if you're not extremely intentional about applying what you've read in these pages, you will miss the investment opportunity of a lifetime.

The Rich Man Who Lost Everything

The poverty-stricken Macedonian believers of the apostle Paul's day were poor men and women who died rich. The parable of a successful businessman, told by Jesus and recorded in Luke 12:16–21, is the story of a rich man who died poor. He missed the investment opportunity of a lifetime.

The wealthy businessman's land had been so productive that he couldn't contain all the fruits of his labor in his existing buildings. After pondering his dilemma for a while, he came up with what he thought was a great solution: build bigger storage facilities where he could protect his gains and take an early retirement. Neither his wealth nor his decision to retire were the issues that made his story so tragic. God has nothing against wealth in and of itself. Scripture clearly tells us it is God who gives us the power to make wealth (Deuteronomy 8:18). God is not against retirement either. Nowhere does He say that people are not allowed to leave their paying jobs for other pursuits. The issue is not wealth or retirement. The issue is what we do with wealth and retirement. Here's what the rich man decided to do: "I'll say to myself, 'You have plenty of grain laid up for many years. Take life easy; eat, drink and be merry" (Luke 12:19).

His wealth and retirement were all about himself. Nothing in what he said indicated a desire to spend his money or time on anyone but himself. But God had the final word and said to him: "You fool! This very night your life will be demanded from you. Then who will get what you have prepared for yourself?" (v. 20). Then God added this chilling warning: "This is how it will be with whoever stores up things for themselves but is not rich toward God" (v. 21). Therein lay the problem: not that the man was rich, but that he had invested his wealth in the wrong place and the wrong person.

A Grave Danger

This was not the first warning associated with the story. Jesus preceded the story with a double warning. "Watch out! Be on your guard against all kinds of greed," He warned. "Life does not consist in an abundance of possessions" (Luke 12:15). Warning number one, "Watch out," carries the idea of *perceiving, thinking deeply,* or *weighing well* the consequences of an action. Warning number two, "Be on your guard," comes from *phylassō*, the Greek word used for a military guard and denotes the idea of *unbroken vigilance.*

Living life for self represents a grave danger—*literally*. It is so great that Jesus gave three words of warning—two at the beginning and one at the end—regarding the overwhelming peril of living life for the wrong thing.

One reason the danger of self-focused living is so great is that it is completely in line with how most people live. If you choose to live for yourself, nobody will notice and nobody will warn you, because so many people live that way. This man was not unusual in his reasoning. He would fit in well with our western society that holds up success stories like his as something to aspire to. The scary thing is that what is true of the world has become true in the church. This man could have attended many evangelical churches today without ever being questioned as to how he was spending his wealth and his life.

A recently retired Christ-follower asked her pastor for advice regarding using her retirement years to advance the gospel amongst the world's least-reached. What he said is so seldom heard in the church, that it bears repeating here:

> Be on guard against being lulled to sleep by a dozen conversations that you're going to have with retired believers who have no dream of making their lives count for the glory of Christ and the suffering of the world. They will be talking about their different toys and their different houses and their different travels

> and their different vacations and on and on and on. And if you're not careful, that's going to start sounding normal. You're going [to] get sucked in and formulate your dreams that way—where the new condo is going to be, how free for yard work you're going to be, how many fun things you can do, and on and on.
>
> Only a mighty work of grace—a glorious work of sovereign grace—can keep you from fitting into the American way of acting as if heaven and all its rest and pleasure begins at retirement instead of death. Heaven begins at death, not sooner.[36]

What Really Defines Life?

The reason God called the rich man a fool is because he was rich in a worthless commodity and he was poor in a priceless commodity. He calls him a fool because he had invested in something which had no future and he had ignored the only thing which did have a future. He had focused on personal gain in this life and had thus forfeited permanent gain in the next.

There are two divine pronouncements made in this passage with which we must come to grips if we ever hope to be rich forever. The first one is captured at the beginning of the story where Jesus said, "Life does not consist in an abundance of possessions" (Luke 12:15b). In other words, *life is not defined by stuff.* Life is not defined by what you have, or what you earn, or what you drive, or what you live in, or where you vacation. Jesus said that, rich or poor, life is not defined by earthly gain.

The problem is that most everyone defines life in those terms, and most everything that goes into that definition is the reality we see every day. We know that people without Jesus will spend eternity in a place called hell, but what we experience day after day is people who look like they're doing fine. They even look quite happy in their pursuit of the American dream. Choosing to forego that dream and invest my time and money to maximize the enjoyment of God's magnificence by as many people as possible demands a huge step of faith.

Eighteenth century American revivalist Jonathan Edwards drafted a series of resolutions as a young man in his twenties and he determined to live by them for the rest of his life. Resolution 22 is:

> Resolved to endeavor to obtain for myself as much happiness, in the other world, as I possibly can, with all the power, might, vigor and vehemence yea violence, I am capable of, or can bring myself to exert, in any way that can be thought of.[37]

Such a statement is so counter-cultural it seems to border on the absurd. Who would ever live like that? Only someone who genuinely believes life is not defined by what you have in this life.

Edwards obviously believed not only the first, but also the second truth that we also must embrace. Jesus expressed it at the end of the parable: *real life is defined by what you have in death.* It is not what you have in this life that defines real life; it is what you have in death. It's not what you've accumulated on this side of the grave, but what you have laid up in store on the other side. It's as if Jesus said, "Do you want to know what life is all about? Look at death, and then tell Me what you have left. Now who will own what you have prepared?"

Benjamin Franklin, whose image graces the United States $100 bill, once said:

> Money has never made man happy, nor will it. There is nothing in its nature to produce happiness. The more of it one has the more one wants. *Instead of its filling a vacuum, it makes one. If it satisfies one want, it doubles and trebles that want another way.*[38] (emphasis mine)

Many down through history have echoed the same sentiment. German American businessman John Jacob

Astor, who lived from 1763 to 1848 and was one of the wealthiest men of his day, reportedly said shortly before his death: "I am the most miserable man on earth."[39]

Harvard Business School professor Michael Norton, who co-authored *Happy Money: The Science of Smarter Spending*, surveyed average-income earners and high net worth Britons about how much more money they needed to be perfectly happy. "Everybody said two to three times as much money," said Norton. Regardless of how much they earned, their answer was always the same.[40]

Many have recognized in death what most people are too short-sighted to see in life: life is not defined by what you have in life; life is defined by what you have in death. Those who focus the investment of their lives and resources in the wrong place ultimately die empty.

Who Will Have What You Have Prepared?

Do you truly believe life is defined by how we use our resources? Think about it for a moment. Does the way you spend your time, your treasure, and your talent reflect that you wholeheartedly believe what Jesus said in this passage? While most Jesus-followers would say that they believe it, many are in danger of living their lives like they don't. Jesus gave a three-fold warning for good reason.

If you were around in the 1980s, you might remember the name Lee Atwater. Lee wanted to accomplish two things before he was forty. He wanted to direct a successful presidential election campaign. And he wanted to be the head of the Republican party. In 1988, at the age of thirty-seven, he achieved his first goal as the director of George Bush's campaign for President. On election day, he achieved his second goal when Bush offered him the leadership of the Republican National Committee.

Less than two years later, on March 5, 1990, while Atwater was giving a political speech, his left foot began to shake. Within seconds, the whole left side of his body was trembling, and he fell. They rushed him to the hospital where a brain tumor the size of an egg was discovered. The doctors gave him ten years to live if he started treatment immediately.[41]

Though Atwater was in good shape and had a will to fight, he quickly realized that he was losing the battle when a second tumor was discovered. Faced with the likelihood of his death, he wrote these words:

> The '80s were the years of acquiring money, power, prestige. I know. I acquired more than most people.

> But you can get all you want and still feel empty. What power wouldn't I trade to have a bit more time with my family? What price wouldn't I pay to spend an evening with friends? This month [February 1991] marks my fortieth birthday—that deadline I set for achieving my life's goals. I lie here in my bedroom—my face swollen from steroids, my body useless.... The doctors still won't answer that nagging question of mine: "How long do I have left?" ...Some nights I can't fall asleep, so fearful am I that I'll never wake up again.[42]

On March 29, 1991, Lee Atwater died at age forty.[43] He achieved his goals. But were they the right ones? ■

Growing Outside the Box

"Be doers of the Word, and not hearers only" (James 1:22).

1. As you observe the prevailing lifestyles and pursuits of western society, what appears to be its definition of life? In other words, what is life all about for them?

2. In what way does your life—particularly your use of time and money—reflect a conviction that life is ultimately about living with eternity in view?

3. John Piper warns us of the real danger of "fitting into the American way of acting as if heaven and all its rest and pleasure begins at retirement instead of death." In what ways might you be "fitting into" that mindset? What can you do to extricate yourself?

4. Read Luke 16:1–13 in preparation for the next chapter. Jot down what it teaches about how to invest for eternity.

16 POOR MAN, RICH MEN

History right up to the present day is littered with examples of men and women who have missed the investment opportunity of a lifetime—one that maximizes the visibility and enjoyment of God's magnificence—and have entered eternity spiritually bankrupt. Tragically, this is reality for most people who have ever lived.

But it does not have to be that way, especially for those who themselves have had a life-transforming encounter with God through faith in Jesus Christ. There is a way to take whatever God has entrusted to you on earth and to invest it so that it accrues to your eternal benefit—and to the benefit of others. Regardless of whether you are rich or poor in this life, you can make yourself and others unfathomably rich forever.

The Wasteful, Brilliant Business Manager

Jesus once told the story of a business manager who was found by the owner of the company to have been squandering the owner's assets. The owner confronted the manager one day and told him to put his accounts in order because he was finished. The manager realized that, at his age, he was not likely to find another job and was too proud to go on welfare. So, he decided to use his last few days on the job to make a few friends for himself among his boss's clients. He called each one who owed his employer money and offered to reduce their bills by up to 50 percent if they would pay up immediately. You can imagine the goodwill his offer inspired. With a stroke of the accountant's pen, half their debt evaporated into thin air.

According to Jesus, it was a brilliant stroke of genius, for this business manager had used the owner's money to take care of his own future. When he left the company as money manager, he had earned so much favor among the company's clientele that he was amply cared for. Even his boss was impressed. Jesus concluded this parable with, "The master commended the dishonest manager because he had acted shrewdly" (Luke 16:8).

Many people have puzzled over how the master could praise the man he was about to fire—a man who had cost him a lot of money. The misunderstanding stems from not differentiating between the manager's first act and his last. His first act was wasteful. The Greek word used to describe his mismanagement, *diaskorpizō,* means "to scatter" or "to squander" (Luke 16:1). He had been throwing away the owner's money through frivolous spending or poor management and it caused him to lose his job. His last act, however, gaining favor with the owner's creditors by reducing their bills, was described as "shrewd." It means "the ability to discern modes of action with a view to their results." Far from throwing money away, the manager carefully considered how to make the most of his master's wealth, albeit for his own benefit, and he chose the course of action that would maximize the return. That is what the master and, by implication, Jesus, commended.

Who Is Better with Their Money?

Jesus added this comment: "The people of this world are more shrewd in dealing with their own kind than are the people of the light" (Luke 16:8). In other words, when it comes to how they handle money, those who don't know

God are often smarter than those who do. Some have found that statement difficult to accept. How could Jesus say that worldly people who spend their money for their own benefit are more astute with their money than are His own followers? Aren't I a better money manager than people who spend their money on lavish vacations, luxury cars, and the satisfaction of their every desire, good or evil? I am much more restrained in my spending, and I even give some of it to the church and the occasional charity. That's better than spending it all on myself, isn't it?

Jesus said it isn't. Why? Because if your unbelieving neighbors are spending their resources to benefit themselves in this life, they are getting the maximum possible personal benefit they, as unbelievers, can get out of it. They are getting the most bang for their buck here and now. But if you, as a Christ-follower, a *son* or *daughter of light* as Jesus called you (Luke 16:1; 1 Thessalonians 5:5), are not spending your life and your resources for the eternal enjoyment of God, then you are not getting the maximum personal benefit out of it. You are missing out on the investment opportunity of a lifetime. And you are not nearly as financially astute as the person who does not know God.

Turning Debtors into Friends

So how do I use my resources the most astutely? How do I get the maximum potential benefit out of what God has given me to manage? Jesus gave a straightforward answer to that question. Here's what He said: "Use worldly wealth to gain friends for yourselves, so that when it is gone, you will be welcomed into eternal dwellings" (Luke 16:9). Jesus was not talking about earthly friends. He was not saying to be generous with your money so your neighbors will like you. He was talking about friends who could "welcome you into eternal dwellings." He was talking about using your resources—time, money, talent, everything—to help as many people as you possibly can to discover eternal life with God. Simply put, smart managers use the Master's money to turn His debtors into friends.

Spending eternity with God in heaven, rather than separated from Him forever in hell, is so gloriously wonderful that helping a single human come to know Him and enjoy Him forever is worth infinitely more than any other way you could possibly spend your time or money. The great British preacher C.H. Spurgeon once said this about the value of a single soul:

> If there existed only one man or woman who did not love the Savior, and if that person lived among the wilds of Siberia, and if it were necessary that all the millions of believers on the face of the earth should journey there, and every one of them plead with him to come to Jesus before he could be converted, it would be well worth all the zeal, labor, and expense. If we had to preach to thousands year after year, and never rescued but one soul, that one soul would be full reward for all our labor, for a soul is of countless price.[44]

Two Widows Who Made Many Rich

The story Jesus told of the widow who put her last two coins into the temple treasury is another example of a poor person who made others rich (Mark 12:41–44). Jesus noted that her gift of two small copper coins was greater than any of the sums the wealthy donors had put into the offering that day. Giving is not so much about the size of the gift as it is about the size of the sacrifice. If the value of her gift in God's eyes dwarfed the actual monetary value of the coins, then it stands to reason that the return on her investment may also have been disproportionate to the actual sum of money. God loves to multiply the return on our investment especially when we give sacrificially. Don't underestimate the impact of a sacrificial gift, no matter how large or small.

During the 1960s in Calgary, Canada, lived a young man burdened to share the gospel in India yet without resources to do so. A church allowed him five minutes during their meeting to plead for support. Afterward, a woman approached him. This mother of five shared that her husband had just died and, in spite of her desperate situation, she offered the young man her entire life savings: $2,000.

That sacrificial gift, along with others, enabled this young man to get to India. Through the ministry he started, two young Indian men who had not yet turned eighteen came to know Jesus Christ as Lord and Savior.

One of the two, Sunder Krishnan,[45] later immigrated to Canada where, for thirty-six years, he pastored with great fruitfulness, the church to which my family and I belonged while living in Toronto. His exposition of Scripture remains among the best I've ever heard.

You will probably recognize the name of the second young man to accept Christ: Sunder's best friend and future brother-in-law, Ravi Zacharias.[46] Ravi also immigrated to North America and later established a ministry that, even after his death in 2020, continues to touch millions of people all over the world.

That poor widow's gift has made countless others rich. Did she have any idea of the legacy and the worldwide impact that would come from that simple, sacrificial gift? Probably not. Only God can give that kind of return on investment.

The Ultimate Example of Generosity

Jesus never told us to do anything He himself did not model. So, we should not be surprised that He led the way when it came to using His wealth to turn debtors into friends. Jesus invested the riches of heaven in such a way as to make many people rich forever.

When the apostle Paul cited the exemplary generosity of the Macedonian believers, he reminded his readers of an even greater example than theirs—the example of Jesus Himself. "For you know the grace of our Lord Jesus Christ," said Paul, "that though he was rich, yet for your sake he became poor, so that you through his poverty might become rich" (2 Corinthians 8:9).

The extent to which the Son of God emptied Himself of His eternal riches—the honor, the glory, the worship, the magnificence of heaven—is something we will not come close to understanding in this life. As Creator God, He was rich beyond imagination. Yet, He chose to become poor—leaving heaven's glory to be born the son of a peasant couple in Roman-occupied Palestine. As if that wasn't enough, He willingly submitted Himself to the indignities of being rejected by the very human beings He had created, and ultimately being executed by them.

Why did He do that? Why did He go from rich to poor? The apostle Paul said it was so that we, His creation, could become rich. The implication of that statement is that we were poor—not materially poor, but spiritually poor and bankrupt. The Bible said, "you were dead in the trespasses and sins in which you once walked… and were by nature children of wrath" (Ephesians 2:1–3, ESV). God created us for life in relationship with Him, but because of our willful disobedience we were destined for death and separation from Him forever in a place called hell.

Thankfully, God was not only rich in terms of heaven's glory, He was rich in mercy towards us. He did not give us what our sins deserved. "But God, being rich in mercy, because of the great love with which he loved us… made us alive together with Christ… so that in the coming ages he might show the immeasurable riches of his grace in kindness toward us…" (Ephesians 2:4, 5, 7, ESV). By means of Christ's death on a cross, and His resurrection from the dead three days later, humanity can become unfathomably rich forever in a place called heaven.

The Best News of All

And here's the best news of all: it's absolutely free. You do not have to earn God's favor. You do not have to merit God's gift. In fact, you *cannot* earn it. It's not for sale. It's free. The Bible said, "For by grace you have been saved through faith. And this is not your own doing; it is the gift of God, not a result of works, so that no one may boast" (Ephesians 2:8–9, ESV). This is what the Bible calls *the good news*, but it's only good if you take it.

Suppose you have terminal cancer, and I have the cure. I think you'd agree that's good news! But it's only good if you accept the cure. Merely knowing there's a cure for the thing that is killing you won't help you one bit. Only when you personally appropriate the cure does it become good news for you.

The way we appropriate God's generous offer of forgiveness and eternal riches is through faith. That simply means we get it by believing God when He says it can be ours. Faith is simply opening our hearts in acceptance of

God's eternal gift, much like we open our hands in acceptance of a physical gift.

My assumption is that most of those who will read this book have already accepted that unfathomable gift of eternal life. If, however, in reading this, you realize you have never opened your heart and mind to accept by faith God's free gift of forgiveness to you, I urge you to stop and do it right now.

Maybe you'd like to express your acceptance of salvation with the following prayer to God. You can say it word for word, or in your own words.

> Heavenly Father, right now I accept by faith the gift of forgiveness and life through Your Son, Jesus Christ. I believe He died for me, to take the punishment I deserved for my sins against You. I believe that three days after He was buried, You raised Him back to life to prove that His sacrifice for me was acceptable to You. Thank you, Father, for forgiving me and giving me the gift of eternal life, through Jesus Christ. Amen.

If you have just now expressed to God your acceptance of His free gift to you, through faith in His Son, Jesus Christ, I'd like to welcome you to His family. You might like to mark this moment in your life by noting today's date as your spiritual birthday in this book, inside the cover of your Bible, or on a calendar. If you use a virtual calendar, make this a recurring annual event to remind you of your decision.

Your name:________________Today's date: ______________

Would You Trust an Unhealthy Doctor?

If you were once a poor man who has been made unfathomably rich, if you have encountered a God who is magnificent beyond imagination, if you have discovered a purpose and a treasure that makes everything else pale by comparison, the best way to convince others is to live accordingly. People do not believe what you say if you don't live like you believe it. This is especially true when it comes to what we say about God.

A few years ago during my annual physical, my doctor told me I had a couple of health issues that needed the attention of a specialist. I had hearing loss and I appeared to have some heart problems. So, he sent me to an audiologist and a cardiologist.

When I arrived for my appointment with the audiologist, I was surprised to discover that, though he was only in his mid-forties, he was wearing hearing aids. He explained how his mild hearing loss hindered his ability to interact with his wife and young children. That's why he had decided it was worth the minor inconvenience of hearing aids to improve his quality of life and relationships. Because his practice clearly lined up with what he said, I was disposed to listen to his advice. As it turned out, I didn't yet need hearing aids. But I can guarantee you that when I do need them, he's the guy I'll go to.

A few days later I went to see the cardiologist. Again, I was surprised when I walked into his office. This time, however, it was for a different reason. The man was about 100 pounds overweight. *This guy looks like a heart attack waiting to happen!* The doctor was pleasant and seemed to know a lot about heart disease. After talking with him for a while, he assured me that he saw many patients with much worse numbers than I had and, as long as I wasn't having any symptoms, I didn't have much to be concerned about.

I left his office that day with a rather unsettled feeling. Could I trust an obese cardiologist who said I didn't have anything to worry about and told me to not come back unless I had chest pains or shortness of breath? I wasn't so sure. Perhaps he was right. He seemed knowledgeable enough. But the fact that his practice didn't seem to align with his profession did not instill confidence.

Live Like You Believe It

If we want people to believe Jesus is the supreme, all-satisfying focus of our lives, we must live like He is. If we want them to believe life is not about what we have in life, but about what we have in death, then how we live must reflect that reality. Pastor John Piper said it so well:

> Finishing life to the glory of Christ means finishing life in a way that makes Christ look glorious. It means living and dying in a way that shows Christ to be the all-satisfying Treasure that he is. So it would include, for example, not living in ways that make this world look like your treasure. The world is not impressed when Christians get rich and say thanks to God. They are impressed when God is so satisfying that we give our riches away for Christ's sake and count it gain.[47]

It's what Jesus did for our sake. And it's what He invites us to do for His sake. "And he died for all, that those who live should no longer live for themselves but for him who died for them and was raised again" (2 Corinthians 5:15). ■

Growing Outside the Box

"Be doers of the Word, and not hearers only" (James 1:22).

1. What did you learn from Jesus's story of the shrewd money manager that surprised or enlightened you? What did you learn that troubled you?
2. List as many ways as you can think of that a person could use earthly wealth to make friends for themselves in heaven (i.e., help people hear the good news about Jesus and come to know Him).
3. If God did an assessment of how you have been managing His resources, would He find you have been wasting His possessions or would you be praised for using it well to turn His debtors into friends?
4. In what way do you think you may be wasting His possessions? How will you change that?

17 DON'T FUMBLE THE HANDOFF

When God told the rich man in Luke 12 that his number was up, He asked him a sobering question: "Now who will get the things you've accumulated?" (Luke 12:20, ISV). It was not a question the rich man had expected to be facing so soon. He anticipated living many more years to enjoy the wealth he'd accumulated. But his life didn't have an expiration date printed on it, guaranteeing a certain number of days. Neither does yours or mine.

Though most of us don't plan on dying anytime soon, some of us will. Since none of us know when we may leave this life, it's important not only to manage God's resources well today, but to ensure, as best we can, that whatever we may leave behind when we're gone continues to be used well to advance His interests.

The Greatest Wealth Transfer in History

Over the next thirty years, the greatest wealth transfer in the history of the world will take place. Estimates are that between $30 trillion and $68 trillion will change hands as the baby boomer generation, those born between 1946 and 1964, passes away.[48] According to some estimates, this represents at least 70 percent of all disposable income in the United States.[49] If we are to use the more conservative estimate of $30 trillion, that's the number 3 with thirteen zeros after it. To put it another way, baby boomers have enough collective wealth to give every man, woman, and child in America $100,000 each. No wonder boomers are called "the wealthiest generation in American history."[50]

What do boomers plan to do with all that money? It's an incredibly important question, especially for those who see themselves as managers of resources entrusted to them by God. There are three primary options for where this wealth could end up.

Let the Good Times Roll

Some of it will be spent by those who decide that it's time to "live a little." Perhaps you've seen the bumper sticker: "I'm spending my kids' inheritance!" Some of these drivers mean it. One survey of 1,000 grandparents between the ages of fifty and seventy revealed that "one in six planned to spend it all before they die." Another study of the same age group indicated that only 40 percent intend to make bequeathals, while 30 percent intend to blow it all before they die.[51]

Second, for those who plan to leave an inheritance, the success of that venture is far from assured. *Forbes* magazine reports that 70 percent of intergenerational wealth transfers will tank.[52] That is, almost all inherited wealth will be spent or squandered within two years of being received.[53]

The Greatest Missed Investment Opportunity Ever

The third option, and one which is overlooked by a huge majority of those who are preparing to hand off their wealth, is to include in their last will and testament a charitable bequest. According to Russell James, planned giving advisor and professor at Texas Tech University, between 5 percent and 6 percent of Americans age fifty-five or older include a charity in their will. This means about 95 percent of Americans—*practically all of them*—are ignoring all charities of any kind.[54]

Unless something changes, this could represent the greatest missed investment opportunity of a lifetime. The 71.6 million baby boomers in America[55] have been entrusted by God to manage trillions of dollars of His assets, and most of them plan on leaving nothing to further His interests.

What About My Kids?

Those who don't spend it all before they die will apparently leave their wealth to their children, grandchildren, or some friend or family member. The idea of not doing so seems almost unthinkable—so unthinkable that, of those who have prepared their wills, roughly 95 percent have not included a charity of any kind, either intentionally or by neglect.

But why *not* leave everything to family or friends? Doesn't the Bible itself say "A good man leaves an inheritance to his children's children" (Proverbs 13:22a, ESV)?

While there are valid reasons to leave a portion of our possessions to the people we love, there are also compelling reasons not to leave them everything and to consider including worthy kingdom causes in an estate plan.

First, this verse in Proverbs is not intended as a prescription for estate planning. The second half of the verse, stated in contrast to the first, said, "But the sinner's wealth is laid up for the righteous" (v. 22b). If we are to conclude that the first half of the verse means believers should leave their money to their grandchildren, then we would have to equally conclude that the second half means unbelievers leave their money to righteous people. Since unbelievers don't generally do that, then we need to understand the first half differently as well.

The verse needs to be read and interpreted as a whole. It is a general statement about the relative value of what one leaves behind. Godly people leave much of value to those who come after them, not the least of which is the treasure of a life well lived. The wicked on the other hand, even if they are wealthy in the world's goods, leave nothing of lasting value to their heirs. In the end, anything ungodly people might do that outlives them will be to the benefit of the righteous who will ultimately inherit the earth.

Wealth Obtained Hastily

But there's a much more important reason for thinking twice about leaving everything we have accumulated to our children: dropping that much money in their laps may actually hurt them. Not only do they risk burning through it quickly, as statistics seem to bear out, but the sudden abundance may rob them of something much more valuable than the inheritance.

David Green is the founder of Hobby Lobby, with 37,000 employees and more than $5 billion in annual revenue.[56] Speaking of the danger of giving too much wealth to family members, he said, "When you have wealth, the hardest thing to do for your kids is not to do." That is, not do for them what they need to learn themselves by hard work. He went on to say:

> I know the feeling of guilt that comes over us when we watch them struggling financially. It's hard not to jump in and ease the pain. If we do, though, we will stunt their development.... Barbara and I have had to say this to our kids and grandkids: "We love you dearly. Part of that love is to arrange things so that you get only what you earn by working. We're going to give you something greater than wealth, which is opportunity. You are most welcome to work at Hobby Lobby if you wish, provided you do a good

> job like anyone else. Then you can enjoy the fruit of your labor. But the ownership of this company is a whole different matter....[57]

Though the Greens could easily set their children and grandchildren up for life with the wealth that has come from a prosperous business, they have chosen not to out of concern that it will hurt them far more than help them. David said:

> I simply don't believe that unearned money helps grow the kind of responsible, motivated, focused offspring we all desire. We simply must raise kids and grandkids to be independent. Otherwise, we make cripples out of them. I don't want any family member to have a choice on whether to work. Every one of them needs to go to work. I will not take that incentive from them.[58]

Randy Alcorn concurred. He wrote:

> Nanci and I will leave to our daughters only enough to be of modest assistance, but not enough to change their lifestyles or undercut their need to plan and pray.... Leaving a large inheritance to children is not just a missed opportunity to invest in God's kingdom. It's also rarely in the children's best interests.[59]

The Value of Hard Work

This is not just the opinion of David Green or Randy Alcorn. Scripture itself teaches the critical importance of hard work. "Lazy hands make for poverty," wrote Solomon, "but diligent hands bring wealth" (Proverbs 10:4). The same chapter in Proverbs that spoke of leaving an inheritance to succeeding generations said this: "Wealth gained hastily will dwindle, but whoever gathers little by little will increase it" (Proverbs 13:11, ESV). We don't do our children and grandchildren a favor by dumping too much money on them. We may be setting them up to waste the second half of their lives taking it easy like the rich man in Jesus's parable planned to do.

I'm not suggesting that we give them nothing. I'm suggesting we think carefully before giving them everything.

Work is not a curse. It is a God-given means to rule over God's creation and to glorify Him. It is a way for us to occupy ourselves fruitfully. It is an opportunity to interact with other human beings who need to encounter Jesus. It is a great teacher of self-discipline, character, responsibility, and more. I do not want my generosity in death to become an unintended obstacle to my children by causing them to depend more on me than on God and His gift to them of fruitful labor.

It is human nature to appreciate something more when we've worked hard for it. David Green's son, Mart, shares that in high school he was disappointed when his dad wouldn't buy him a car. He had to work for it. Looking back on the experience, Mart observed, "Looking around at my high school and college friends, I could just about tell you which ones had paid for their car themselves by how they drove it! You take better care of something you worked for." [60]

The Gift of a Lifetime

One final reason to consider seriously including a local church, mission, or kingdom-minded ministry in an estate plan is that it represents what, for some, will be the single greatest gift they will ever make. During our lives, we may strain to give more than a few thousand dollars a year to the cause of spreading the gospel, but it's possible our final gift could reach into the tens or hundreds of thousands of dollars. The cumulative impact of that kind of giving is hard to imagine. Imagine that just 10 percent of the $30 trillion that will change hands in the next thirty years is currently in the possession of Christ-followers. If they were to give just 10 percent of those resources to advance the gospel worldwide, it would equal $300 billion—more than 100 times more than what is currently allocated in any given year to world missions by the North American church.

Our Daughter Charity

God has blessed us with four delightful adult children, four more as they each married, and twelve grandchildren as of the publication of this book. None of our children is independently wealthy, but all four families have good jobs, good health, a roof over their heads, and God willing, many more years of fruitful life and work ahead of them.

How much do they need in terms of additional income? I'm sure they would appreciate some extra money to pay down the mortgage on their houses. It might be wise to start saving money for the college education of their kids. But do they *need* more money? Not really. For the time being at least, they're all doing fine.

So, a few years ago, Jerusha and I decided to welcome a fifth child into our family. Her name is Charity. Actually, she's been part of the family all along. We provided for her from the first day of our marriage through giving to our local church and to global missions. Over the years, Charity became an increasingly big portion of our budget.

A few years ago, we also decided to include her in our last will and testament, along with our four other children. Rather than splitting our inheritance four ways, we decided to split it five ways, with Charity receiving one part. Will our children be worse off because we've chosen to include Charity as one of the beneficiaries of our estate? I don't think so. If they're doing fine now, chances are they'll be doing just fine whenever we might exit this life in the next thirty years.

As the years go by, we will likely rebalance the designations of our estate plan based on the needs of our family, the size of our estate, and our desire to invest as much as we possibly can in things that will last forever. What we will not do is assume our children need it all. If they have needs, we will certainly do our best to help them. But as managers of someone else's possessions, our first consideration is not what might be nice for our family, but what best advances the interests of the One who owns that which we're managing.

Where Races are Won or Lost

In the 4x100 meters relay, the most critical part of the race takes place in the changeover box, that twenty-meter stretch of track where the baton is handed off from one runner to the next. Races are won or lost in that box. While running at nearly top speed, both runners must seamlessly transfer the baton while looking straight ahead and staying in their lane.

At the 2008 Olympics in Beijing, the American men's and women's relay teams were both favored to medal. Yet neither of them did. All their speed and excellence in running well counted for naught because they failed in the handoff.[61]

The greatest handoff of wealth in the history of the world is upon us. Running well as managers of God's resources is good, but what a shame it would be to drop the baton in the transfer. ■

Growing Outside the Box

"Be doers of the Word, and not hearers only" (James 1:22).

1. "My family members should be the sole recipients of my assets when I'm gone." Do you agree or disagree with that statement and why?
2. What factors are the most important to you in determining what people or causes you include in your estate plan?
3. Why do you think so few people, even believers, include charities in their estate plan?
4. How should the belief that we are managers (not owners) of God's property affect whether we prepare a will, and who we name as the beneficiaries of our estate?
5. Read John 12:1–8 in preparation for the next chapter. What do you learn about generous giving?

18 LET THE PARTY BEGIN

The blessing of God on those who are generous is so great that it should inspire us to celebration. What's more, God's Word teaches that part of the whole giving experience involves personally enjoying some of the benefits of God's provision for us.

As I shared in an earlier chapter, I have at times been guilty of stinginess when it comes to my own family, giving them less than I should out of a desire to give more to the work of God. Realizing my need to demonstrate generosity to my own family if I hope for them to embrace a generous lifestyle, I have sought to build special times of celebrating

God's goodness into our lives. One of the ways we do that is through an annual celebration dinner.

This idea first came to me years ago when I was reading through the Old Testament and came across these words in Deuteronomy 14:22–23. There God said to His people:

> "Be sure to set aside a tenth of all that your fields produce each year. Eat the tithe of your grain, new wine and olive oil, and the firstborn of your herds and flocks in the presence of the LORD your God at the place he will choose as a dwelling for his Name, so that you may learn to revere the LORD your God always."

At first, I thought I had misread the passage. *Did God just tell me to eat my tithe?* So, I read it again: "Eat the tithe of your grain...." As I read on further into verses 24–26, God seemed to say it even more explicitly:

> "But if that place is too distant and you have been blessed by the LORD your God and cannot carry your tithe (because the place where the LORD will choose to put his Name is so far away), then exchange your tithe for silver, and take the silver with you and go to the place the LORD your God will choose. Use the silver to buy whatever you like: cattle, sheep, wine or other fermented drink, or

> anything you wish. Then you and your household shall eat there in the presence of the LORD your God and rejoice."

This surprised me! God actually told His people they could use some of their tithe to prepare a celebration dinner for the family to rejoice together in the goodness of His provision. Twice in the passage God emphasized that His people could purchase "whatever your heart desires" (v. 26, NASB) and He would pick up the tab. Interestingly, He adds in the next verse: "And do not neglect the Levites living in your towns…" (v. 27). Lest this should become just one big party, God reminds them that in their celebrating they should not lose sight of the purpose of their giving: caring for God's work and His workers.

A Dinner Worth Remembering

This passage has become the foundation for an annual event in the life of our family that we all greatly enjoy. Around the same time Jerusha and I celebrate our wedding anniversary and do our annual inventory of God's provision, we plan a special family dinner. The purpose is to celebrate God's faithful provision for us over the course of another year. There are several things that set this dinner apart.

First, we choose an upscale restaurant in keeping with the nature of celebration. This is not a Golden Arches event where the kids super-size their order from a wall menu. My favorite so far has been a revolving restaurant overlooking Toronto's lakefront. That dinner was truly a memorable evening complete with steak, seafood, and a spectacular view.

Another characteristic of the evening is that the instructions for dinner are always the same: "Order whatever you want." This aligns with the Old Testament instruction to eat "whatever your heart desires." This has been, admittedly, a challenge for all of us. We don't eat out often and we keep our appetites within reasonable limits which, being translated means, "Don't even think of ordering one of the expensive entrees." We have also learned to have a great appreciation for "water with lemon" when it comes to beverages. So, when we come to our annual celebration dinner, it is hard to convince everyone that "whatever" truly means "whatever," but it does. Even so, we're still quite a restrained bunch.

This meal isn't just "a nice dinner on Jesus," but a celebration of God's goodness in our lives. Because of that, we remind everyone of the purpose and then take some time to recount some of the special ways God has cared for and blessed us over the preceding twelve months. When one of our children graduated from university debt-free, we celebrated. When my wife and I marked a milestone anniversary with a long-awaited trip to Hawaii, we celebrated God's goodness in that. We also talk about how God has enabled us to bless others through various ministries and people we support. We recall some of the special people God has brought into our lives as a family to bless us. Each year, the evening is truly a time of rejoicing in the God who richly supplies us with all we enjoy.

Such a Waste

Some might conclude this is needless waste. How could we possibly condone spending so much money on a meal and paying for it out of the tithe? First, it's God's idea, not mine. I would never have dreamed of doing it if God Himself hadn't suggested it. Second, one dinner per year represents only a tiny portion of our overall giving that year. Finally, the focus of the celebration has never been enjoying a meal at God's expense, but rather enjoying God. Personally, I think He is honored by that much in the same way He was honored when a certain woman in Scripture "wasted" a lot of money frivolously on a bottle of expensive perfume.

You may remember the story. Just days before the Lord Jesus's crucifixion, He visited the town of Bethany, having dinner in the home of a man "known as Simon the Leper" (Mark 14:3). A woman, identified in the apostle John's account as Mary, the sister of Martha and Lazarus, approached Jesus with an extremely expensive bottle of perfume and, breaking the seal, anointed His head and feet with it, using her own hair to wipe it from His feet. Both Mark and John mention the perfume was valued at roughly 300 denarii, equivalent to an entire year's wages for a common laborer. Based on today's wages for an entry-level worker, the perfume was worth an estimated *$35,000!* [62] This was no ordinary bottle of perfume.

Though I love Jerusha dearly, I have never spent more than $100 on any bottle of perfume. It's not that I don't like perfume, and it certainly is not that I don't love my wife deeply. It's just that, to me, expensive perfume is a luxury item—an extravagance that, no matter how sweet the fragrance, is to be indulged in sparingly.

How did Mary come to have such an expensive perfume in her possession? Perhaps she had purchased it to be used in anointing her brother Lazarus for his burial. Then, in the confusion and grief of their mourning as they waited for Jesus to arrive and save their brother, the perfume had gone unused. When Jesus then raised her brother from the dead, Mary used it on Jesus out of deep love and gratitude.

Another possibility is that she had wanted to buy the perfume for Lazarus's burial but had resisted, knowing how much she and her sister Martha would need the money to survive as single women. Then when Jesus raised her brother from the dead, the economic threat vanished, and Mary decided to purchase the perfume as a lavish expression of her love for her Savior.

Whatever the case may be, clearly this woman was so overwhelmed with love and gratitude for Jesus that no sacrificial expression of love was too great. But most of those who were present that evening did not share her views. They considered her action an extravagant waste. They used the Greek word *apōleia*, translated *waste* in English, which is the same word used to describe the eternal loss of destruction in hell. What a thing to say about someone's gift to Jesus! Mark noted the onlookers' indignation as they talked among themselves and then, unable to contain their irritation over such a wasteful act, "they rebuked her harshly" (v. 5), suggesting the money would have been better spent on some charitable activity.

That's when Jesus intervened with a harsh rebuke for her critics, telling them to lay off their attacks because "she has done a beautiful thing to me" (v. 6). What others saw as wasteful, Jesus saw as "beautiful." The Greek word for that, *kalos*, is variously translated *beautiful, handsome, excellent, eminent, magnificent,* or *admirable.* What a contrast in viewpoints. Others saw it as a damnable act of lunacy, but Jesus saw it as an admirable act of love.

Jesus's point was clear: no act of worship no matter how costly is wasted when Jesus is the focus of that worship. He was so impressed that He went on to make this amazing statement: "Truly I tell you, wherever the gospel is preached throughout the world, what she has done will also be told, in memory of her" (v. 9). Imagine that. Mary's act of so-called "wasteful" worship would be forever memorialized right next to the worldwide preaching of the gospel.

My purpose in relating this amazing account of sacrificial giving is two-fold. First, it illustrates that any act of Christ-centered worship, whether it be a bottle of perfume or a roast beef dinner eaten in His honor, is a beautiful thing in His eyes. God loves it when we celebrate His glorious, delightful character. Second, Mary's example serves as a powerful reminder that we all have much room for growth when it comes to our giving. Her giving was not merely exceptional, it was extravagant in the extreme. Mine, by comparison, still has a long way to go. ■

Growing Outside the Box

"Be doers of the Word, and not hearers only" (James 1:22).

1. Read God's instructions to His people in Deuteronomy 14:22–26. What surprised you about this?
2. How does the concept of giving as celebration compare to each of the following passages?
    - 1 Chronicles 29:9
    - Deuteronomy 12:5–7
    - 2 Corinthians 8:1–4
    - Malachi 1:13
3. What value could there be in taking time to celebrate God's generosity in this way?
4. Consider planning an annual dinner celebrating God's generosity to you. Where might you go to celebrate it? Think of the people and ways He has used this past year to show you His generosity.

19 TRUST GOD AND PULL THE LEVER

The preponderance of the Bible's teaching on giving seems to indicate that contributing a tenth of our income back to God is a great place to start a journey in giving. If the statistics are even close to accurately capturing the giving habits of the average Christ-follower, then many believers have barely started on the incredible journey I've been describing. But how does one get started? How do *you* start? For many, 10 percent feels like a huge leap of faith.

Someone might say, "I'm going to start tithing by giving 5 percent of my income." Such a statement is problematic for at least two reasons. First, it is a contradiction of terms because *tithe*, by definition, is 10 percent. How can someone give 10 percent of their income by giving 5 percent?

In Canada, a mock political party began in 1963 called The Rhinoceros Party.[63] Fueled by satire, their credo was "a promise to keep none of our promises." They ran on a platform of outlandish pledges designed to entertain the voting public. One was a plan to switch from driving on the right-hand side of the road to driving on the left. They proposed, however, that in order to help with the transition, they would phase in the new system in stages. For the first month, only trucks would switch to the left side.

While giving a half-tithe may not be so deadly as a half-transition to driving on the left, it may demonstrate a lack of understanding about the critical role of faith when it comes to giving. Giving away that which we legitimately need is not primarily a matter of self-discipline. It's a matter of faith.

Taking a Leap of Faith

There is no easy way to begin the journey of obedience in giving other than to do it by faith. Faith is believing God and what He says and acting accordingly. Faith is *not* about believing God to do what we think He should do. You may have heard people say, "I have faith to believe God is going to heal me." That may sound like faith, but it's not. God is *able* to heal, but He is not obligated to heal just because someone thinks He will. Biblical faith is believing that God is trustworthy and that no matter what He chooses to do, I can trust and obey Him.

Exercising biblical faith in your giving also means you stop doing things you cannot afford. A faith decision to start giving may mean a parallel faith decision to stop overspending. It may mean moving to a smaller house, driving an older car, or cutting up your credit cards. Stepping out in faith in the matter of grace giving does not mean we can blindly ignore other necessary financial decisions, as if God will somehow magically multiply our dollars simply because we've written the tithe into our budget. We must put ourselves in a position where our decision to trust God in the matter of giving is not sabotaged by a failure to exercise discipline and sacrifice in the matter of spending.

The decision to embark on the journey of giving must never be predicated on whether we think we can afford it. Biblical faith means believing what God has said and acting accordingly, even if it seems humanly impossible. I realize that, for those who have given little or nothing in the past, the prospect of *starting* by giving 5 or 10 percent of their income to God may seem as far-fetched as walking on thin air. Remember, however, that while God gave no commands or promises about walking on thin air, He did make Himself quite clear in the matter of giving and His commitment to bless those who obey Him. That may not make it easier, but it does make it safer! Faith is a requirement for living a life that pleases God. "Without faith," we are told, "it is impossible to please God, because anyone who comes to him must believe that he exists and that he rewards those who earnestly seek him" (Hebrews 11:6). There's that word again: *reward*. God rewards a life of faith. And God will reward the one who, by faith, chooses to obey Him by getting started in giving.

A Death-Defying Act

I have never been much of a daredevil when it comes to extreme sports. Rappelling backwards off cliffs and walking across wires strung 100 feet above solid ground have never held much appeal for me. My children, on the other hand, are a different story.

Years ago, we were visiting a familiar theme park in Texas when the friend with us offered me $100 if I'd take a particular ride that featured being dropped in a freefall from 200 feet up, tethered to the end of a crane. Attached in a body harness, lying face down, its riders would fall for about 100 feet before swinging out in an arc that would send them rocketing over the heads of the spectators below. I declined the offer and had hardly gotten the words out of my mouth when one of our kids piped up that they'd be glad to accept the challenge, money or no money.

Minutes later, Jerusha and I watched our son along with two of his friends being winched up into the clouds and left to hang until they pulled the release lever that would send them hurtling towards the ground. Were we crazy? If we wouldn't do it, why would we let our own flesh and blood? Simply this: We had confidence the cable and harness would not fail. We had seen enough riders sail safely over our heads to believe our children would be okay. We just didn't relish the heart-stopping freefall.

When it was all over and the daredevils were safely back on the ground, we asked them what the most difficult part of the experience had been. Their answer? "Pulling the release lever."

If you've never done it before, stepping out in faith with regard to giving generously of your income may feel like a death-defying act. Yes, others have done it and survived, but how can it possibly work for you? The key to pulling the release lever of giving is to have confidence in the One who has put this whole thing together. He is more trustworthy than any human being who has ever lived. He has never been wrong, never made a mistake, and never failed those who trust Him. But like the amusement park ride, there is no way to ease yourself into obedience. You simply need to trust Him and pull the release lever.

Opening the Windows of Heaven

After I had preached a message on biblical giving, a man came to me and said, "I've tried it and it doesn't work." He quoted to me the passage from Malachi where the prophet exhorted the Israelites to bring God the whole tithe and test His ability to open the floodgates of heaven in response. This gentleman went on to say he had tried tithing, but God hadn't come through. This was the first time I'd heard anyone say this. I had heard many testify to how God has provided for all their needs in response to their obedience in giving, but I had never had anyone tell me God hadn't come through.

It is impossible to respond to a statement like that without knowing more of the background. I do not know what circumstances led this man to draw the conclusion he did. Unfortunately, he did not want to take the time to get together and discuss it. Neither do I know what he meant by "didn't come through." He still had clothes on his back and food in his belly. He looked healthy and to be gainfully employed.

I may never know what that man meant, but I can tell you on the authority of God's Word, and from my personal experience, that God never breaks His promises. The overwhelming testimony of Scripture is that God multiplies His blessing on those who honor Him with their resources. This does not mean He always does it immediately. It does not mean He always pays us back in the same currency as what we have given. It certainly does not mean we will never go through lean or difficult times. But I know God can be trusted to do what He says He will do.

You Can Count on God

God may not act when or how I think He should, but He will always act in a way that is consistent with His character and His Word. When He says He loves a cheerful giver, you can count on it. When He says the one who sows his resources plentifully will reap plentifully, you can count on it. And when He says He will open the windows of heaven and pour out an overflowing blessing on obedient givers, you can count on it. He may not do it tomorrow, or even next month or next year. But He will do what He says He will do. Take it by faith and pull the lever. ■

Growing Outside the Box

"Be doers of the Word, and not hearers only" (James 1:22).

1. How did each of the following acts of obedience require stepping out in faith despite all indications to the contrary?
   - Leviticus 25:18–22
   - 1 Kings 17:8–16
   - Luke 21:1–4
   - 2 Chronicles 25:5–10
2. Think of a time when you stepped out in obedience to God but couldn't see how it could possibly work out. What happened?
3. In what way is your faith being challenged in the area of giving?
4. How does 2 Corinthians 9:8–11 speak to your fears about giving?

20 AN UNFORGETTABLE JOURNEY

The trip Jerusha and I took to Hawaii a few years ago was one that had been in the making for twenty-five years. From our wedding day onward, we had dreamt of going to Hawaii, but at every major milestone it just never seemed practical or affordable. "Sure, it would be nice," we reasoned, "but we really shouldn't spend the money. And who would take care of the children? And what would people think of such extravagance?" The reasons for not going were endless, though not all were valid.

When our twenty-fifth wedding anniversary came and went and we still hadn't made any plans to go, I decided that whatever it took, we would go before another year passed. And we did.

We flew out of Toronto on a cold, snowy January morning and arrived at our hotel in Waikiki beach in time for dinner. It was, without a doubt, the most beautiful, enjoyable journey we had ever taken. The weather, the ocean, the sand, the food, the scenery… everything was incredible. It was hard to believe we were on the same planet as the cold, snowy one we had left behind in Toronto. I only wish we hadn't waited twenty-five years to do it. Since then, we've made up for our delay and have gone two more times.

What Hawaii has been to our journeys on earth, giving has been to our journey with God. We have experienced a world we would never have imagined if we hadn't embarked on the journey of learning to give outside the box. It has been without a doubt one of the most spectacular journeys of our lives. The promises of God's Word concerning the delights of honoring Him with our resources have not been exaggerated. His goodness to us has surpassed anything we could have anticipated. There have been times when we felt like we could ill-afford the giving journey, yet invariably the benefits of embarking on this faith venture have by far exceeded the investments made.

What, you might ask, have been the highlights of the journey, the sights you wouldn't want to miss? Let me summarize for you just a few of them.

Highlight 1: Supernatural Provision

It has been amazing to experience *God's supernatural provision* in response to our giving. God's intervention in the financial affairs of our lives has often caused us to sit back in wonder at His activity. While we realize that God is under no obligation to always give us more of His abundance, our experience has generally been that He does just that. Somehow, year after year, we find that no matter how much we give, we are not worse off for it. We can't out-give God. Over the years He has provided everything from pencil cases to real estate and many things in between.

One of those in between gifts from God occurred when we had been saving up to purchase a used vehicle. After three years of socking away cash in a car fund, we had about $13,000 saved and I was eager to find the minivan I'd been dreaming of. One morning as I was praying that

God would give me wisdom in picking out the right vehicle, I sensed Him prompting me to pray in another direction. As I prayed, I said: "Lord, you know I'm getting eager to make this purchase, but if You have some other way that You wish to provide for this need, please help me to be patient long enough for You to show me."

That day I had a lunch meeting with a friend who was a retired businessman in the city where we lived. As we wrapped up our lunch and prepared to part ways, he said, "There's just one more thing that I need to talk with you about. I had a call this week from someone who wishes to remain anonymous and would like to give you the funds for the purchase of a new vehicle." I could hardly believe my ears. I was thoroughly amazed, not only at the unexpected provision of God, but at His incredible timing in prompting me to pray as I had that morning and in keeping me from running ahead of His plans. Rather than purchasing a used vehicle with the money I had saved, God provided, through a very generous friend, a brand new minivan that we drove for the next fifteen years. *Supernatural provision* is certainly one attraction you will be sure to see if you embark on this journey.

Highlight 2: Contentment

Another amazing part of the journey that you don't want to miss is the *contentment* that comes as a byproduct of giving. It is not by accident that one of the primary biblical passages addressing the issue of contentment is the apostle Paul's letter to a group of generous givers. Writing to the believers in Philippi who had so generously given of their resources to the missionary endeavor, Paul acknowledged that he had known times of great abundance as well as times of great need. Then, summing it all up he wrote, "I have learned to be content whatever the circumstances… I have learned the secret of being content… whether well fed or hungry…" (Philippians 4:11–12).

I'm not sure I could say with Paul that I *have* learned, but I can certainly say that *I am learning* this secret. It honestly does not bother me to drive an older car. My current vehicle will soon be ten years old, and the one I retired before this one was fifteen. Could I afford to buy a new one? Yes, I could. But my old one suits me just fine. Most days, I'm truly content with it.

I don't lose sleep over under-performing investments. I have no desire to buy the latest piece of technology when it hits the market. Jerusha, even more than me, seems to be genuinely happy with whatever she has. She is one of the most content people I have ever met. I have never felt pressure from her to earn more money, and even though she rarely spends money on herself, she never gives the impression she needs anything.

Paul not only said he had learned contentment with having little; he also said he had learned the secret of contentment with abundance. That's harder than you might think, especially if you've been raised with the unbiblical notion that wealth is bad and should be hidden. I find myself sometimes having to fight the temptation to explain to people why I have something of quality—as if it's only spiritual to live in a pleasant home or drive a newer car if I can demonstrate it was a huge bargain or a gift from someone. We have friends in vocational ministry who are incapable of saying they went out to a nice restaurant without adding that they "had a coupon for it." Contentment with abundance means, among other things, not having to justify to people when God allows me to have more than I deserve (which, to be truthful, is all the time).

How do we learn to be content with little or much? A big part of the answer lies in learning to be a more generous giver. The more we give, the more we are freed from the desire to have more stuff and from the temptation to hide it when God blesses us with extra. It's one of the many amazing attractions on the journey of giving.

Highlight 3: Increased Giving Capacity

It's amazing to me how seldom Jerusha and I have felt tapped out in our giving. Rarely have we felt like we have reached our limit. A few years ago, we were winding down one of the most expensive periods of our lives, having had one or two children in university every year for ten years straight. Yet somehow, even in that financially demanding stretch of the journey, we didn't feel as if we couldn't give any more. By God's grace we maintained our local church as our number one giving priority, we helped our children with the costs of their schooling, lived generously toward those around us, and not only maintained but increased our financial commitment to the spread of the gospel worldwide. I am not boasting as if we did something great. We didn't. God did. It is God who increased our capacity to give and God who gave us the resources to meet the commitments we made and the needs we had. We experienced God's promise, "You will be enriched in every way so that you can be generous on every occasion" (2 Corinthians 9:11).

Highlight 4: Joy and Freedom

Money and possessions can become a terribly enslaving preoccupation. An appetite for material things can easily become like saltwater—the more you drink it, the thirstier you get. On the other hand, money rightly used can be the source of great joy and freedom. The more we have learned to release the resources God has entrusted to us, the more we have experienced this reality. Not only has it brought us joy and freedom, but we have experienced that same joy and freedom when it comes to talking to others. I have few inhibitions when it comes to telling others why they should embark on the journey of becoming increasingly generous givers.

Highlight 5: Discovery of Truth

I've also found an unusual joy in discovering biblical truth I never knew was there. This has been particularly true when it comes to what God says about giving and receiving. I never imagined there was so much in the Bible that touched on this subject. And the more I ponder it, the more I see and the more excited I get. God's Word is invigorating. As David once wrote, it truly is "more desirable than gold, yes, than much fine gold; Sweeter also than honey and the drippings of the honeycomb" (Psalm 19:10, NASB).

Looking Back

What started fifty years ago as my five-minute Sunday morning ritual with the little, red, tin box above the stove has become one of the most wonderful journeys imaginable. How I thank God for parents who had the foresight to teach me about giving, both by word and by personal example. Though they are now almost ninety years of age and living off the modest retirement income of a small-town pastor, they continue to be extremely generous people.

I also thank God for that day back in 1981 when God clearly spoke to Jerusha and me through His eternal Word, ultimately moving and enabling both of us to respond to His challenge to begin giving outside the box. Not once in all these years has He ever failed or disappointed us in the matter of giving and receiving.

Taking Up the Challenge

Regardless of where you are in your stage of life or your journey in giving, I'd like to lay before you a challenge: to grow in the grace of a generous life—to follow in the footsteps of Him who, though eternally rich, became temporarily poor so that we through His poverty might become eternally rich. God did not make us temporally rich so that we could hoard wealth, but so that we could make poor men, women, and children rich eternally.

If you have not yet taken the faith step of giving 10 percent of your income back to God, I would urge you to get started. Don't wait until you think you can afford to do it. Giving has nothing to do with affordability and everything to do with faith. If debt, poor money management, or a materialistic lifestyle is an issue, seek out a godly financial counselor and deal with it now. But whatever you do, don't keep short-changing God and hurting yourself.

Regardless of what you've been giving up to this point in your journey, ask God how He wants you to grow in generosity in the coming year. Make this an annual event. You may want to use the two simple questions Jerusha and I have asked: First, has God been faithful this past year to meet all our needs when we gave Him *x* percent of our income? And second, can we trust Him in the coming year to increase our giving to *y* percent?

When you have set your goals, get started right away. Make your gifts to God your first financial priority each month, not the last, so that it doesn't end up being spent on something else. Giving God the first of our increase is not only a way to honor Him, it's an effective way to ensure we are able to keep our commitment.

Don't expect it to be easy right away. As with any discipline, starting can often be the most difficult step. But the more you exercise that muscle, the stronger it gets, and the greater your capacity becomes.

Use It, Or...

The late Jacques Lowe was a photographer whose images of the John F. Kennedy family most of us would recognize. Careful to preserve his precious negatives in a fireproof bank vault, he never sent anyone to retrieve them when a museum or magazine wanted prints. He went himself. The vault contained about 40,000 negatives worth more than $2 million dollars. But all of that changed on September 11, 2001, as the contents of the fireproof vault containing his irreplaceable treasure were reduced to ashes along with everything else contained in the World Trade Center where he kept his negatives. In a few horrifying seconds of time, it was all gone, never again to benefit anyone.[64]

It is human nature to stockpile treasure, to seek to preserve today's excess for tomorrow's needs. The problem, however, is that since we don't know how many tomorrows we may have, it's hard to know how much excess we should keep. If we hang on to too much for too long, we risk losing it all, along with the ability to invest it in ways that will preserve it for eternity.

Think about this analogy from Randy Alcorn.

> Have you ever played one of those card games where the winner is the one who runs out of cards first? At the end of the game, every card left counts against you. The American dream is to die with as many cards in your hand as possible. But maybe we've got it backwards.[65]

When God calls "last card" signaling that the game is almost over, I don't want to be left with cards in my hand. Like the shrewd manager whose boss told him his time was up, I want to invest God's resources in such a way that heaven will be filled with friends who will welcome me and thank me for a hand well played.

May God help you to live your life in such a way that when life is over, you will be eternally and unfathomably rich and will take many others along with you. ■

Growing Outside the Box

"Be doers of the Word, and not hearers only" (James 1:22).

1. What have been some of the highlights of your own giving journey?
2. What truths of Scripture have most impacted your thinking and behavior about giving?
3. How are you doing with learning the secret of contentment?
4. How will you put into practice something you've learned about God's invitation to grow in the grace of giving?
5. Consider making it an annual practice to review your financial giving from the previous year and to set a goal for the year ahead. Ask yourself these two questions:
    - Has God been faithful this past year to provide for all my needs when I gave him *x* percent of my income?
    - Can I trust God by increasing my giving in the coming year to *y* percent?

EPILOGUE:
YOUR GREATEST ASSET

This chapter is not an afterthought. It's an extension of the message of this book on exceptional generosity. But this chapter—an epilogue, if you will—is different. It's about stewardship of one's whole life.

As I articulated at length in chapter 14, the ultimate purpose of life is the eternal enjoyment of God's glory by those whom He created. Everything we do should be devoted to that purpose. This is what the apostle Paul meant when he said, "So whether you eat or drink or whatever you do, do it all for the glory of God" (1 Corinthians 10:31). "Whatever you do" covers everything—not only how we spend our money, but how we spend our leisure time, how we parent, how we treat our spouse, how we choose our entertainment, how we do our job. The list is as long as our choices in life. Doing all of that "for the glory of God" means doing it in a way that maximizes the visibility and enjoyment of His magnificence.

Missing A Great Investment Opportunity

I love a great investment. About ten years ago I decided to take 10 percent of what I had in my tax-deferred retirement account and invest it in Microsoft stock. I've regretted that decision ever since. If you know anything about how that stock has performed in recent years, you may be surprised that I'd say I have regretted it. Here's why. I have not regretted buying the stock. What I have regretted is investing only 10 percent of my portfolio in that stock. For in the ten years since I purchased it, the stock has grown by over 700 percent. How I wish now that I had invested more.

Many believers are missing out on the incredible investment opportunity of using their wealth for God's glory and the eternal joy of themselves and others. But there is another investment opportunity. It may be life's greatest when it comes to maximizing the visibility of God's magnificence to a watching world, yet untold millions of Christ-followers seem to be missing it.

What is it? You may be surprised by my answer. It's not our wealth. It's our work. Not our possessions, but our *professions*. It's what we spend most of our lives doing. It's the source of much of the financial income we've been talking about stewarding well. And sadly, it is for many the greatest missed investment opportunity of all. We can give God 10 or 20 or 30 percent of our income, yet we can still fail to recognize the potential kingdom investment opportunity our work itself offers. That's like investing only a fraction of our life portfolio in a stock whose returns will dwarf all others—forever.

Disciple-Makers from All Professions

When I became the president of Crossworld back in 2009, I and my fellow leaders became convinced we'd been missing out on a huge kingdom investment opportunity.

Up until that point in our ministry's eighty-year history, most of the people we had sent to the nations had been vocational missionaries—people like myself who had gone to Bible college and seminary, joined a mission organization, and raised financial support to do full-time ministry in another part of the world.

But what about the rest of the body of Christ—the other 99 percent who worked as professionals in the secular marketplace? Had not God called them to full-time ministry too through their jobs? When He said, "whatever you do, do all for the glory of God" (1 Corinthians 10:31), did that not include the thing they spent the majority of their waking hours doing? Convinced that indeed it did, we changed course.

Instead of mobilizing only vocational missionaries to go to the nations, while telling the rest of the body of Christ they could simply "stay, pray, and pay," we began to dream of "disciple-makers from all professions bringing God's love to life in the world's least-reached marketplaces."

Second-Class Citizens?

Jesus did not recognize two classes of believers—those who are "called to ministry" and those who are not. He did not view life as a sacred-secular dichotomy as we have in western Christianity where everything the pastor and missionary does is sacred and everything the rest of us do is secular.

Yet this is often how we have portrayed it. Ask any Christ-follower to describe what ministry they are involved in, and they will almost invariably talk about what they do for thirty minutes on Sunday morning or an hour on Wednesday evening: teaching a class of eight-year-olds, leading a small group, or parking cars between services. Almost never do they speak of their profession as ministry. But it is. As already noted, the apostle Paul said whatever we do is to be done for the glory of God. That sounds like ministry to me.

In another place, writing to a large group of workplace believers, Paul said, "Whatever you do, work heartily, as for the Lord and not for men, knowing that from the Lord you will receive the inheritance as your reward. You are serving the Lord Christ" (Colossians 3:23–24, ESV). Did you notice that word *whatever* again? *Whatever* covers every profession God may assign to us. And the apostle clearly said that through our profession, whatever it may be, we are working *for the Lord.* In case the reader had a hard time believing it, Paul said it again explicitly—"You are serving the Lord Christ."

Called to Full-Time Ministry

If you are a doctor, you are serving the Lord Christ. If you are a software designer, you are serving the Lord Christ. If you are a barista, a taxi-driver, a sales manager, a stay at home parent—you are serving the Lord Christ. Whatever passion God has put in your heart, whatever profession He has put on your resume, and whatever instrument He has put in your hand has been put there as a means of making His magnificence visible to a watching world. You are called to full-time ministry through your profession.

Maybe you're thinking, "Not my profession! There's no way I can serve God through my lousy job! There's no way I can make an eternal investment out of what I do."

In some cases, it may be that you're in the wrong profession. If so, you need to figure out how God has uniquely wired and gifted you and then move into the work God has called you to. But in most cases, it's not a matter of leaving your job but of leveraging it for His glory—of realizing God is calling you to full-time ministry through that job.

You might be interested to know that the workplace group Paul addressed in this passage was the lowest of the low on the scale of workplace professions: slaves. Many slaves had horrible bosses, horrible pay, and horrible working conditions. And even to them he said, "You serve the Lord Christ" (Colossians 3:24, NKJV).

Your work is not merely a means of putting food on the table and paying the bills. Your work is a call to full-time ministry. You have an opportunity to rub shoulders with lost people who may never have another viable opportunity to get a glimpse of what Jesus is like. Sometimes we leaders in the church and mission world have wrongly attributed to ourselves the designation of "full-time ministry" as if it were our exclusive domain. How many times have I heard pastors or missionaries say things like, "I left my job in business when God called me to full-time ministry"? Where does that leave the rest of the body of Christ? What does it communicate to them? Whether intentional or not, it communicates that they are not called by God and that their work is not ministry. It's a job. That's all.

Listen to what Paul said about the politicians of his day:

> Let everyone be subject to the governing authorities.... For the one in authority is God's servant for your good. But if you do wrong, be afraid, for rulers do not bear the sword for no reason.

> They are God's servants, agents of wrath to bring punishment on the wrongdoer.... This is also why you pay taxes, for the authorities are God's servants, who give their full time to governing" (Romans 13:1, 4, 6).

Did you catch what Paul said about them—not just once, but three times? They are God's servants (some translations say *ministers*). And then he adds, "who give their full time to governing." According to Paul, even politicians are in full-time ministry. They are God's full-time servants. If that is true of politicians, and if it is true that slaves also "serve the Lord Christ" (Colossians 3:14, NKJV), then it is true of all of us, regardless of our profession. We are all called to full-time ministry through our work.

Business Professionals in Full-Time Ministry

I went to visit Bill a few years ago when we at Crossworld were beginning the journey of engaging business professionals in our vision to reach the nations. I had heard of his missional business in a large Asian city, but I was not prepared for what I encountered. From the moment he met us in the parking lot of his company, his lips dripped godly wisdom. Everything he said about his work in manufacturing seemed to be seamlessly interwoven with Scripture. He'd be speaking about suppliers and balance sheets and logistics, and the next thing you knew he'd be connecting it with some biblical truth. And it wasn't corny or offensive. It was natural and attractive.

I was particularly interested to meet this man because I had known his brother Tom who had served for many years in Europe as a vocational missionary. Each of them had a unique, God-given wiring. Each leveraged his skills for the glory of God—full-time. And each saw significant spiritual fruit—Tom as an evangelist and church-planter, and Bill as the employer of hundreds of workers, many of whom came to faith in Christ through his influence.

More recently I met Brian who works internationally for an American company that does all its manufacturing in Asia. Brian is clearly a businessman. He's a skilled engineer for the company. He is also a godly servant of Christ who has a zeal to see life in that country transformed for God's glory. The company invests in the growth and well-being of their employees and of the community around them. They are well-known by the local government as a company that gives back to the community. And through his life and work, Brian and several of his co-workers have been used by God to start and lead a new fellowship of

Christ-followers. For Brian, life is not bifurcated between work and ministry. It is an integrated whole.

The Two Go Hand in Hand

Your work is every bit as much a kingdom asset to be invested for eternal benefit as your money is. Work is not a curse. It is a blessing. It is not to be squandered; it is to be stewarded. It is not to be avoided; it is to be invested. It is not a waste; it is an act of worship. God is calling you to a life of exceptional generosity through your work. If you'd like a better understanding of what that looks like, you might enjoy a book I wrote on this topic, *A Better Way: Make Disciples Wherever Life Happens.* My purpose in mentioning it here is not to sell more books, but rather to help you make the most of an incredible investment opportunity—the investment of your God-given profession.

Remember Zacchaeus

Zacchaeus certainly made the most of his profession. Do you remember his story? It's in Luke 19:1–10. This little rich man, hated by all, encountered Jesus and was so transformed that he did two unfathomable things: he gave away as much as 90 percent of his wealth, and he kept his job as a tax-collector. If anyone should have quit his job to go into "full-time ministry," it was Zacchaeus. His was a dirty and despised profession. He was reviled by his contemporaries for having sold out to the Romans by collecting the taxes they imposed on their conquered subjects. He was hated not only for being a so-called traitor but also for being crooked—taking more money from taxpayers than he was supposed to take in order to pad his own bank account. He admitted as much when he said to Jesus, "If I have defrauded anyone of anything, I restore it fourfold" (v. 8, ESV). This was not a claim of innocence. It was more of an admission and a commitment to right the wrongs he had done.

Neither Jesus nor Zacchaeus gave any indication that he should leave his profession as a tax-collector. Far from leaving his profession for ministry, Zacchaeus seemed intent on leveraging it for ministry. Monday morning was going to be radically different for him and his customers. No, he wasn't going to start preaching to them instead of collecting Roman taxes. He was going to treat them with honesty and respect. He was going to be the most trustworthy, God-fearing tax-collector they had ever known.

I can just imagine him showing up at the door of the Leventhal family on Monday morning and saying: *Good morning, Mr. Leventhal. I've come by to make something right. Last year I taxed you a thousand dollars more than I should have. This past weekend I met Jesus, and He's changed my life. Here's a check for $4,000 in compensation for the wrong I've done you. Have a great day and God bless you.* Wouldn't you love to go to work with the transformed idea of customer service Zacchaeus had? Even more, if you had to pay your taxes, wouldn't you want to pay them to a collector like him?

I would argue that far more powerful than Zacchaeus's exceptional giving was his exceptional living. He lived out the gospel through his work in such a way that those who encountered him were never the same. The world needs a few more believers like Zacchaeus. It needs men and women of faith and virtue who have been transformed by the power of the gospel to flood the marketplaces of the world to live and love like Jesus among people and in places that I, as a vocational religious worker, could never access.

Zacchaeus was a rich man who, like Jesus, voluntarily became a poor man, so that others through his poverty might become rich.

What about you? What riches has God entrusted to you?

For many, it's financial wealth that, by global standards, easily puts us amongst some of the richest people in the world, if not in all of history.

For many others, it's your profession—a career that allows you to live out the gospel day in and day out next to people who desperately need the life that you've been given.

And for all of us who know Jesus, it's Jesus Himself. In Matthew 13, His kingdom is like the "treasure hidden in a field" (v. 44) and like "beautiful pearls" (v. 45, KJV). Upon finding that treasure, that pearl of great price, the finder "went and sold all that he had and bought it" (v. 46). What an investment to make—everything he had. *But oh, what a return!*

And now it's up to you. What is God asking you to do with the resources He's entrusted to you? What would it look like for you to take your riches—your time, talent, profession, and possessions—and intentionally invest them for His glory so that others through your sacrifice might become rich—forever?

"For you know the grace of our Lord Jesus Christ, that though he was rich, yet for your sake he became poor, so that you through his poverty might become rich" (2 Corinthians 8:9). ■

Growing Outside the Box

"Be doers of the Word, and not hearers only" (James 1:22).

1. Why do you think Jesus didn't seem to urge Zacchaeus to leave his profession for a "higher calling"?
2. Read Luke 3:10–14. What strikes you about Jesus's advice to tax-collectors and Roman soldiers?
3. Re-read 1 Corinthians 10:31, Colossians 3:22–24, and Romans 13:4–6. What do those passages have to say to you about your work?
4. To what extent have you understood your profession to be a God-given call to full-time ministry? How well are you currently experiencing that reality?

ADDENDUM

FREQUENTLY ASKED QUESTIONS

1. Does the New Testament require believers to give 10 percent of their income to God?

The short answer to this question is no. But a one-word answer is both incomplete and misleading.

The question itself is not the right one to ask. It would be a bit like a married man asking, "Now that I'm married and no longer engaged, do I have to keep taking my wife out on dates?" Though the answer to the question might technically be no, it begs another question: "If you really love your wife, why would you even ask that question? Do you want to stop taking her out on dates?"

The New Testament does not require believers to give 10 percent of their income. But a true understanding of grace and the magnitude of God's love and forgiveness inspires us to give more, not less. Jesus made this clear in an encounter He had with a Pharisee and a woman who lived in the same town. Though the woman had a reputation for living a sinful life, she went to the house where Jesus was having dinner with the Pharisee. "As she stood behind [Jesus] at his feet weeping, she began to wet his feet with her tears. Then she wiped them with her hair, kissed them and poured perfume on them" (Luke 7:38).

The religious leader severely criticized the woman for her act and Jesus for allowing her to even touch Him. Jesus responded by pointing out that her gesture to Him was borne out of love and gratitude, while the Pharisee's attitude towards Jesus left much to be desired. Then Jesus concluded with these words: "Whoever has been forgiven little loves little" (Luke 7:47).

When we've experienced the incredible grace of God, we are not required to give a certain amount, but we are inspired to give as much as we possibly can. If we are growing givers, that will probably exceed 10 percent.

2. What if, for whatever reason, I simply can't afford to give much money to kingdom endeavors like the church or global missions?

First of all, let me repeat: There is no required amount that we must give. So we can set aside the feelings of guilt. God does not want us to give out of guilt. He loves joyful, willing, heart-felt giving.

Second, giving is generally not a question of affordability. It is true that many people can ill-afford to give, and for many different reasons. Low earnings, unemployment, unexpected expenses, college expenses, sickness, and more can reduce our financial margin to zero or even push us into negative territory.

An apparent inability to give is often the greatest reason why we *should* give. In a sense, those who can't afford to give can't afford *not* to give. Why? Because God loves to provide for those who are generous. Giving when we can least afford it is an act of faith God loves to honor.

Multiple times in Scripture, God commends and provides for those who are poor but give anyway. The widow of Zarephath would have died if she had not given her last piece of bread to Elijah (1 Kings 17). The widow in the gospels who gave the last two coins she possessed was commended by Jesus (Luke 21:1–4). Certainly He would not have commended her if He had thought it ill-advised. And the poor believers in Macedonia begged for the opportunity to give in spite of the fact that they could not afford to (2 Corinthians 8:1–5).

3. What if my spouse is not in favor of giving? Should I give anyway?

Probably not. Money is one of the leading sources of marital conflict and breakup. It is important, as much as it is possible, to avoid financial decisions that ignore a spouse's opinion.

I would suggest first that you seek to have an open dialogue on the matter—perhaps even suggesting a trial period to the dissenting partner. If you can, agree together to give a certain amount and then assess whether you are better or worse off for the experience. If God wants you to give, He is more than capable of passing the test.

I think of Daniel and his three Hebrew friends when they arrived in the court of an unbelieving foreign king. They didn't want to eat food forbidden by their religious convictions, so Daniel asked for a trial period to see if the four of them could be as healthy eating their own food as those who ate the king's food. At the end of the trial, they actually proved to be healthier than their peers. You can read the full account in Daniel, chapter 1.

Ultimately, God knows your heart. If you long to give, He knows that. If He wants to change your spouse's heart, He can do that. Relax and let Him do the heavy lifting.

4. How much of my giving should go to my local church versus other charities and needs outside the church?

There is no set amount one should give to the local church. But since Christ loves the church, I want to make it the highest priority in my giving. My personal conviction is that I begin by giving a tithe (10 percent of all my income) to my local church. Any giving above and beyond that I give to whatever causes or needs God lays on my heart. That could be for the support of a cross-cultural worker, a local non-profit ministry, a friend or neighbor in need, my community, the poor, or additional giving to my local church.

If you are already giving to worthy causes outside of your local church, and are not giving at least 10 percent to your church, I would not advise dropping your other commitments. But I would advise that, as you grow in your giving capacity, you make it a priority to increase your giving to your church.

5. Should I tithe on my gross income or my net income?

Since grace giving is more about generous, joyful, faith-inspired giving than it is about meeting the requirements of the Law, the question of gross versus net income becomes somewhat irrelevant. I simply want to give as much as I can and continue to grow in my giving.

But if you're just getting started in the journey of becoming a growing giver, and you want to establish a baseline for what 10 percent looks like, my personal conviction is to use gross income as the baseline. I don't remember where I heard it, but someone asked, "Do you want God to bless your gross income, or just your net income?"

6. Is there a tax benefit for charitable giving?

Tax laws related to charitable giving differ greatly from country to country and change on a regular basis. In

Canada and the United States, there are currently ways to give that can significantly reduce your tax obligations depending on your age, income, and other factors. For example, stock gifts or gifts from an individual retirement account, can, in some cases, carry greater benefits than cash gifts. A skilled financial advisor can help you discover the best ways to maximize the impact of your giving.

7. Isn't the level of giving advocated in this book something for those who have the gift of giving and not necessarily for all believers?

There does appear to be a spiritual gift of giving (Romans 12:6–8). A person with this gift may be more apt to give generously than one who does not possess this gift. But that does not mean only those with the gift of giving should be growing givers.

The apostle Paul exhorted all believers in Corinth to "excel in this grace of giving" (2 Corinthians 8:7). In an earlier letter to them, speaking of an offering being collected for poverty relief, he said, "each one of you is to put aside and save" (1 Corinthians 16:2, NASB) for the collection. It was not only those with the "gift of giving" who were expected to give. It was everyone.

But the most compelling answer to this question is the disposition of God toward those who give. He loves givers. He loves to bless givers. He makes a multitude of promises about generous giving. So, whether I have the gift of giving or not, if I believe what God says about giving, I'll want to get involved.

8. Does God guarantee He'll return to us as much or more than we give away?

No, He doesn't. The false teaching of prosperity theology—that God will make you financially prosperous if you give your wealth to kingdom pursuits—is nowhere taught in the Bible. It is a dangerous, deceptive teaching.

The Bible makes it clear that if God chooses to prosper a person financially, it is not to make him or her rich, but to enable even greater generosity.

God's Word also makes many statements about His love for and commitment to bless those who are generous with the resources entrusted to them, but He does not promise when or how He will do that. He may repay us in a different "currency" than the one we give. He may multiply our joy. He may bless us with the fruit of people coming to faith through our generosity. And yes, He may entrust additional material wealth to those who are generous managers of His resources.

The general teaching of Scripture about giving is that God loves to bless those who honor Him with their wealth—not to enrich them, but to advance His kingdom.

9. How do I decide how much money I keep and how much I give?

You are correct that you have to decide. God does not tell you how much you must give. He gives you the freedom to make those decisions, all the while urging you to be generous and to trust that He will take care of you when you honor Him with your wealth.

But the fact is that your wealth is not yours. It's His. You are only the manager. So, while you have the freedom to choose how you will use His resources, you will also be responsible to give an account to Him, the Owner, of how you have managed His estate.

That is what should guide our decision-making. When I give an account to Him someday for how I managed His property, will the car I chose to drive and the house I lived in and the vacations I took—at His expense—be justified? I can't answer that for you. But you will have to give an answer to God. Jesus's story of the wasteful manager seemed to indicate that the day will come when each of us will leave this life and He will say to us, "Give an account of your management, because you cannot be manager any longer" (Luke 16:2). I try to make my choices now, in light of that day.

10. Can you get to the point where you've grown all you can in your giving?

I don't know. I know I haven't gotten there yet, even after being on this journey for over 35 years. I hope I'm still growing in faith, in love, in patience, and in the many other desirable qualities of a Christ-follower. I hope I can keep growing in this one too. ■

Meet Dale

Dale Losch *(lawsh)* begins each day with a cup of coconut flavored coffee, a square of dark chocolate, and his Bible. His story begins as a pastor's kid in Canada. From then until his newlywed days with Jerusha, Dale conscientiously tithed of his income. When the young couple heard a new perspective on giving, it changed their lives. He says, "Growing in the grace of giving frees us from a materialistic focus and has increased our capacity to respond quickly and joyfully to new giving opportunities."

This book springs from Dale's early writing to his children about the joy of generosity. He draws on his formal education (a bachelor's degree in Missions from Christian Heritage College in El Cajon, California, and a master's degree in Theology from Dallas Theological Seminary in Dallas, Texas), his decades of pastoral and cross-cultural ministry, and his real-life experience as a husband, father, and friend. Dale is also the author of *A Better Way: Make Disciples Wherever Life Happens.*

One of the things Dale enjoys most in life, besides spending time with his wife, his kids, and their twelve (and counting) grandchildren, is sharing biblical truth with everyday relevance so that people can discover life as it is meant to be.

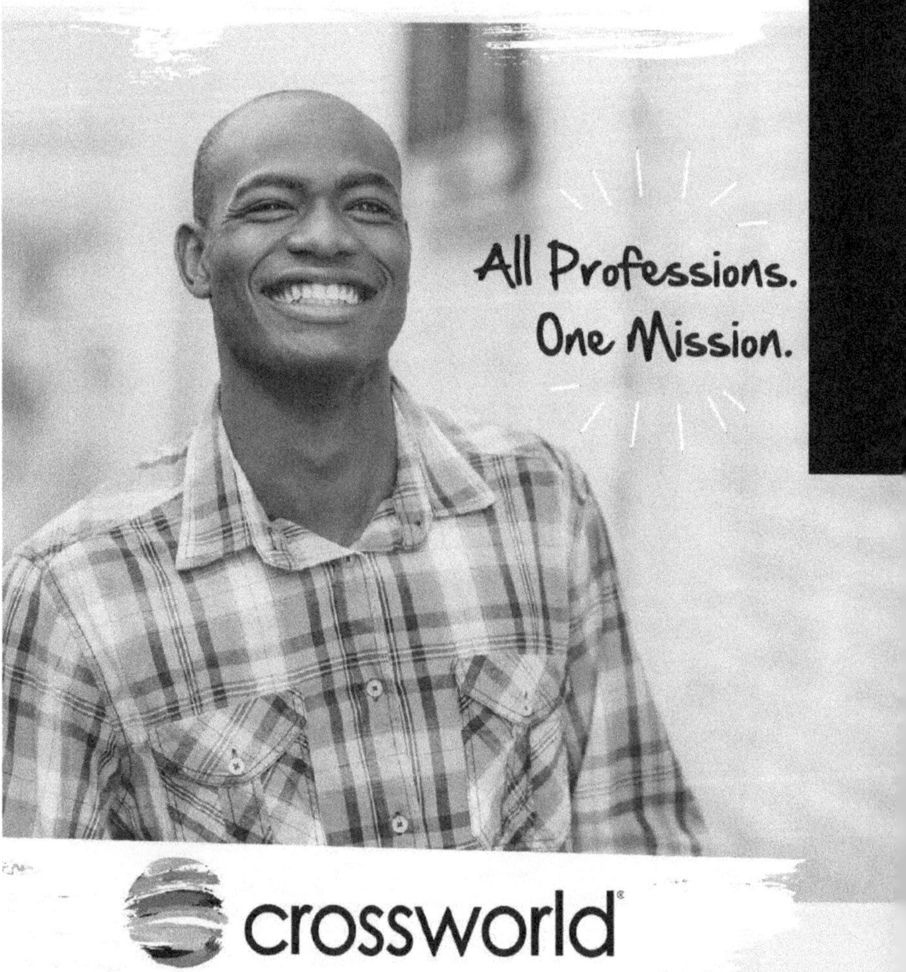
All Professions.
One Mission.

NOTES

Preface

1. Michael B. Sauter, Samuel Stebbins, “How the Current Stock Market Collapse Compares with Others in History,” *USA Today*, March 21, 2020, https://www.usatoday.com/store/money/2020/03/21/stock-market-collapse-how-does-todays-compare-others/2890885001/.

Chapter 1: The Story of the Red Box

2. Ruth Moon, “Are American Evangelicals Stingy?,” *Christianity Today*, January 31, 2011, https://www.christianitytoday.com/ct/2011/february/areevangelicalsstingy.html.

Chapter 2: Is It Really More Blessed to Give?

3. Janine Puhak, “Plane passenger gives first-class seat to 88-year-old woman, makes her 'dream' come true: 'No one asked him to,” *Fox News,* December 16, 2019, https://www.foxnews.com/travel/plane-passenger-first-class-seat-woman.

Chapter 3: Why Are We So Blessed?

4. "Percentage of American's who believe their financial situation is 'at least somewhat' reflective of 'God's regard' for them: 70," *Harper Magazine* (October 1995), accessed July 1, 2020, https://harpers.org/archive/1995/10.

5. Howard Taylor, *Hudson Taylor and the China Inland Mission: The Growth of a Work of God* (London: The Religious Tract Society, 1919).

Chapter 4: Money Wars

6. Dave Ramsey, "Money Ruining Marriages in America," *Ramsey Solutions,* February 7, 2018, https://www.daveramsey.com/pr/money-ruining-marriages-in-america.

Chapter 6: Raising the Bar on Generosity

7. Randy Alcorn, *The Treasure Principle: Unlocking the Secret of Joyful Giving* (CO: Multnomah, 2001), 3.

8. Ashley May, "A Christian polytechnic university takes after its inventive founder," *Philanthropy Round Table,* Summer 2017, https://www.philanthropyroundtable.org/philanthropy-magazine/article/ summer-2017-building-builders.

9. Ron L. Jones, *Jesus, Money, and Me: Discovering the Link Between Your Money and Your Faith* (New York: iUniverse, Inc., 2004), 100.

10. Joe Mellor, "Poor People Really are More Charitable Than the Rich According to New Research," *The London Economic,* June 28, 2018, https://www.thelondoneconomic.com/news/environment/poor-people-really-are-more-charitable-than-the-rich-according-to-new-research/28/06/.

Chapter 7: Taking Off the Training Wheels

11. Alcorn, *The Treasure Principle,* 65.

Chapter 8: Is It Really More Blessed to Give?

12. Charles R. Swindoll, *The Grace Awakening Devotional: A Thirty Day Walk in the Freedom of Grace* (Tennessee: W Publishing Group, 2003), 164.

Chapter 9: When You Can't Afford to Give

13. Alcorn, *The Treasure Principle*, 67-68.

Chapter 11: The Generosity Killer

14. Jeff Cox, "Consumer Debt Hits New Record of 14.3 Trillion," *CNBC*, May 5, 2020, https://www.cnbc.com/2020/05/05/consumer-debt-hits-new-record-of-14point3-trillion.html.
15. Megan Leonhardt, "Here's How Much Debt Americans Have at Every Age," *CNBC*, August 20, 2018, https://www.cnbc.com/2018/08/20/how-much-debt-americans-have-at-every-age.html.
16. Northwestern Mutual, "Planning and Progress Study 2018," *Northwestern Mutual*, December 11, 2018, https://news.northwesternmutual.com/planning-and-progress-2018.
17. Bruce Howard, "Borrowing Trouble?," *Leadership Journal*, October 1, 2002, 54-55, https://www.christianitytoday.com/pastors/2002/fall/7.50.html.
18. Philip A. Clemens, "Choosing Contentment – a Personal Story," *The Center Consulting Group*, 2019, https://static1.squarespace.com/static/571fc0ea1d07c0fd6d72c167/t/5ca60da471c10b273e31326d/1554386341091/choosing-contentment-philip-a-clemens.pdf.

Chapter 12: Is God Opposed to Wealth?

19. Kristine Owram, "Toronto lawyer sentenced to 39 months in prison for insider trading scheme," *Investment Executive*, January 8, 2010, https://www.investmentexecutive.com/news/from-the-regulators/toronto-lawyer-sentenced-to-39-months-in-prison-for-insider-trading-scheme/.
20. John Bunyan, *The Whole Works of John Bunyan* (UK, Blackie: 1862), 737.
21. Gil Student, "Saving one person is like saving the world," *The Real Truth about Talmud* (blog), http://talmud.faithweb.com/articles/schindler.html.

Chapter 13: Don't Eat that Marshmallow...Yet

22. Jessica McCrory Calarco, "Why Rich Kids Are So Good at the Marshmallow Test," *The Atlantic,* June 1, 2018, https://www.theatlantic.com/family/archive/2018/06/marshmallow-test/561779/.

    Keith Payne and Paschal Sheeran, "Try to Resist Misinterpreting the Marshmallow Test," *Behavioral Scientist*, July 3, 2018, https://behavioralscientist.org/try-to-resist-misinterpreting-the-marshmallow-test/.

23. Bruce Wilkinson, *A Life God Rewards: Why Everything You DO Today Matters Forever* (Colorado: Crown Publishing Group: 2002).

24. Erwin W. Lutzer, *Your Eternal Reward: Triumph and Tears at the Judgment Seat* (Illinois: Moody Publishers, 2015), 52.

Chapter 14: The Ultimate Purpose of Giving

25. *Shorter Catechism of the Assembly of Divines*, A Puritans Mind (blog), https://www.apuritansmind.com/westminster-standards/shorter-catechism/.

26. Operationworld.org

27. John Piper, *Let the Nations be Glad! The Supremacy of God in Missions. 3rd Edition* (Michigan: Baker Academic, 2010), 35.

28. John Piper, *Don't Waste Your Life* (Illinois: Crossway, 2003), 180.

29. Richard Stearns, *The Hole in our Gospel: The Answer that Changed My Life and Might Just Change the World* (Tennessee: Thomas Nelson, 2009), 217. Emphasis by author.

30. Maurie Backman, "The Average American Spends Almost $18,000 a Year on Non-Essentials," *The Motley Fool,* May 6, 2019, https://www.fool.com/retirement/2019/05/06/the-average-american-spends-almost-18000-a-year-on.aspx.

31. Douglas A. McIntyre, "Ten Things Americans Waste the Most Money On," *24/7 Wall Street,* February 24, 2011, https://247wallst.com/investing/2011/02/24/ten-things-americans-waste-the-most-money-on/.

32. Amy Watson, "North American box office revenue from 1980 to 2019," *Statista,* January 10, 2020, https://www.statista.com/statistics/187069/north-american-box-office-gross-revenue-since-1980/.

33. Colin Dixon, "Consumers taking pay TV, rental, purchase dollars to fund SVOD," *N Screen Media*, January 13, 2020, https://nscreenmedia.com/svod-growth-at-pay-tv-vod-est-expense.
34. Operationworld.org
35. Operationworld.org

Chapter 15: Rich Man, Poor Man

36. John Piper, "I'm Retired and Want to Do Missions — What's My First Step?," *Desiring God,* Episode 1139, December 29, 2017, https://www.desiringgod.org/interviews/im-retired-and-want-to-do-missions-whats-my-first-step.
37. Jonathan Edwards, *The Works of Jonathan Edwards, Vol. 1* (Edinburgh: Banner of Truth, 1976), xx-xxi.
38. Jesse Campbell, "13 things Benjamin Franklin said about money that are still true today," *Money Management,* July 1, 2015, https://www.moneymanagement.org/blog/13-things-benjamin-franklin-said-about-money-that-are-still-true-today.
39. Tim Savage, *Discovering the Good Life* (Illinois: Crossway, 2019), Kindle ch. 3.
40. Melissa Leong, "If Money Doesn't Buy Happiness, Why Are We So Obsessed with Getting More of It?," *Financial Post,* January 10, 2019, https://business.financialpost.com/personal-finance/material-things-dont-define-happiness-so-why-are-we-obsessed-with-money.
41. Lee Atwater and Todd Brewster, "Lee Atwater's Last Campaign," *Life,* February 1991, 61.
42. Atwater and Brewster, 67.
43. Michael Oreskes, "Lee Atwater, Master of Tactics for Bush and G.O.P., Dies at 40," *New York Times*, March 30, 1991, https://www.nytimes.com/1991/03/30/obituaries/lee-atwater-master-of-tactics-for-bush-and-gop-dies-at-40.html.

Chapter 16: Poor Man, Rich Men

44. Charles Haddon Spurgeon, *The Complete Works of C. H. Spurgeon, Vol 34* (Delaware: Delmarva Publications, Inc.: 2003), Sermon no. 2051.

45. Sunder Krishnan, *Hijacked by Glory: From the Pew to the Nations* (2014), 137.
46. Ravi Zacharias, "Ravi Zacharias Tells his Life Story Including His Conversion in YFC," *Youth For Christ International*, October 21, 2014, http://www.yfc.net/about/storiesblog/ravi-zacharias-tells-his-life-story-including-his-conversion-in-yfc/.
47. Piper, *Don't Waste Your Life*, 72.

Chapter 17: Don't Fumble the Handoff

48. MacKenzie Sigalos, "68 Trillion Is About to Change Hands in the U.S.," *CNBC*, November 20, 2018, https://www.cnbc.com/2018/11/20/great-wealth-transfer-is-passing-from-baby-boomers-to-gen-x-millennials.html.
49. Jess Stonefield, "Are Boomers Ready to make the Greatest Wealth Transfer in History?," *Next Avenue*, May 21, 2018, https://www.nextavenue.org/boomers-wealth-transfer/.
50. Sigalos, *CNBC.*
51. Gabriele Garcia, "That $30 Trillion 'Great Wealth Transfer' Is A Myth," *CNBC*, May 22, 2018, https://www.cnbc.com/2018/05/22/that-30-trillion-great-wealth-transfer-is-a-myth.html.
52. Stonefield, *Next Avenue.*
53. Elizabeth O'Brien's, "One in Three Americans Who Get an Inheritance Blow It," *Market Watch*, September 3, 2015, https://www.marketwatch.com/story/one-in-three-americans-who-get-an-inheritance-blow-it-2015-09-03.
54. Tim Hewson, "Planned Giving: the State of Charitable Requests in the US," US Legal Wills, February 15, 2017, https://www.uslegalwills.com/blog/planned-giving/.
55. Richard Fry, "Millennials Overtake Baby Boomers as American's Largest Generation," *Pew Research*, April 28, 2020, https://www.pewresearch.org/fact-tank/2020/04/28/millennials-overtake-baby-boomers-as-americas-largest-generation/.
56. Forbes.com, "Hobby Lobby Stores," https://www.forbes.com/companies/hobby-lobby-stores/#64814b726cee.

57. David Green, *Giving it All Away and Getting it All Back Again* (Michigan: Zondervan, 2017), 110, 112.

58. Ibid, 115.

59. Alcorn, *The Treasure Principle*, 71-72.

60. Green, *Giving It All Away,* 116.

61. Associated Press video report, “Olympics '08: U.S. Relays Fumble Chances,” *You Tube,* August 21, 2008, https://www.youtube.com/watch?v=vQCi3mayB3Q.

Chapter 18: Let the Party Begin

62. Phillip Massey, “Parable of two Debtors,” *Biola University Chimes,* October 27, 2010, https://chimesnewspaper.com/13189/opinions/parable-two-debtors/.

Chapter 19: Trust God and Pull the Lever

63. https://www.partyrhino.ca/en/

Chapter 20: An Unforgettable Journey

64. *Kindred Spirit,* Dallas Theological Seminary, Summer 2004, Vol. 28 No. 2, (Texas) 10.

65. Alcorn, *The Treasure Principle*, 71-72.

Made in USA - North Chelmsford, MA

11.03.2020 1547